GRAPPLING WITH FAITH

DECISION CASES FOR CHRISTIANS IN SOCIAL WORK

TERRY A. WOLFER AND MACKENZI HUYSER

CONTENTS

CONTRIBUTORS

Sandra L. Bauer, PhD, LSW, is the Chairperson of the Social Work Department at Eastern University and teaches in the practice and human behavior sequences. She also works with churches concerning trauma issues and healing.

Sherry Bell is a school social worker for the Jackson Madison County School System in Jackson, Tennessee. She has a BS from Lambuth College and an MSW from the University of Tennessee. She is a Licensed School Social Worker and a Licensed Clinical Social Worker.

Jennifer L. Fahy works as a child welfare analyst with expertise in child protective services and foster care programs. She received her bachelor's degree from the University of Wisconsin-Madison and master's degree from the School of Social Service Administration at the University of Chicago.

Leslie S. Gregory, MSW, LSW, is the Field Education Director at Eastern University and teaches in the practice and social welfare policy sequences. She also works in private practice serving individuals and families.

Nelson Henning serves as Professor and Director of the Social Work Program at Cedarville University. He has experience in: rehabilitation and corrections, child/spouse abuse, mental health, employee assistance, and chemical dependency. He served as a military social worker for more than 20 years before coming to Cedarville University. He received his PhD from the University of Pittsburgh in 1986.

George E. Huff is an Associate Professor of Social Work at Cedarville University, Cedarville, Ohio and an independent licensed social worker. He received his bachelor's degree from Ashland University (OH) and his master's degree in science and social administration from Case Western Reserve University. Before Cedarville, he worked in child welfare for more than 25 years. He was an adjunct faculty member for Ashland University and North Central State College.

Mackenzi Huyser, PhD, MSW, is Chair and Professor of Social Work and Dean for Faculty Development and Academic Programs at Trinity Christian College. Her recent scholarly interests include hospitality as a virtue, intentional Christian communities, and the impact of neighborhood demographic change on Christian institutions. In 2010, she was awarded an Emerging Leader in Social Work Award from the National Association of Social Workers Illinois Chapter.

Christine Kessen, DSW, LCSW, is a licensed clinical social worker with over twenty years of social work practice experience in health, mental health, and school settings. She has presented widely at professional conferences on topics related to ethics, meditation, and social work practice. As an Associate Professor of Social Work at Marywood University in Scranton, Pennsylvania, she teaches graduate social work courses in practice, ethics, psychopathology, and spirituality.

Mary Anne Poe is Professor of Social Work and Director of the Center for Just and Caring Communities at Union University in Jackson, Tennessee. She has a BA from Vanderbilt University, MDiv from the Southern Baptist Theological Seminary, and an MSSW from the University of Louisville.

Clifford J. M. Rosenbohm, ACSW, LCSW, is the Director of the Social Work Program at George Fox University, Newberg, Oregon. He is a Ph. D. candidate at the Mandel School of Applied Social Sciences at Case Western Reserve University. His direct practice work has been primarily in the field of child welfare. His research interests focus on religion and spirituality in social work education and program development and assessment.

F. Matthew Schobert, Jr., LCSW, ACSW, C-SWHC, is Administrative Officer for Social Work Service at the Central Texas Veterans Health Care System. He works with the Chief of the Service to manage social work programs and activities, supervises social work staff in mental health residential and out-patient programs, and directs the Social Work Training Program. He is also a member of the NASW Texas State Ethics Committee.

Michael E. Sherr, PhD, LCSW, is Associate Professor and Director of the Ph.D. Program in the School of Social Work at Baylor University. His work appears in top journals in both social work and Christian education. He is the author of Social Work with Volunteers (Lyceum) and On Becoming a Christian Educator in Social Work (NACSW).

Jeanette Ucci, MSW, is a Social Worker for Westminster Canterbury Richmond, a continuing care retirement community in Richmond, Virginia.

Maggie Wiles, MSW, holds a Bachelor of Social Work degree from Trinity Christian College (2009) and a Master of Social Work degree from Aurora University (2010). She works as a school social worker in DeKalb, Illinois and is a member of the Illinois Association of School Social Workers.

Terry A. Wolfer, PhD (Chicago), MSW (Ohio State), is a Professor of Social Work at the University of South Carolina. He has co-edited or co-authored four previous collections of decision cases, and led faculty development workshops on case method teaching and case writing. In 2009, he was awarded the Distinguished Recent Contribution in Social Work Education Award by the Council on Social Work Education.

Carrie Yocum is the Assistant Provost at Grace College in Winona Lake, Indiana. She received her BS in social work from Manchester College, her MSW from Andrews University, and her PhD in Leadership from the Andrews University School of Education. Prior to working in higher education administration, Carrie worked in the field of community mental health and was the chair of the undergraduate social work program at Grace College.

Laura Zumdahl, PhD, MSW, is the Associate Executive Director at Cabrini Green Legal Aid in Chicago. She has worked previously in social work education and child welfare. Her research interests include nonprofit leadership development, management, and innovation. In 2010, she was named a Chicago Community Trust Emerging Leader Fellow to investigate design thinking and innovation in nonprofit organizations.

INTRODUCTION

GRAPPLING WITH FAITH: DECISION CASES FOR CHRISTIANS IN SOCIAL WORK

Terry A. Wolfer and Mackenzi Huyser

To the Student

This casebook provides a set of decision cases involving religion, spirituality, and faith in social work practice. It represents part of a continuing effort to help you grapple with these matters in your class work and, in turn, to develop sensitive competence in approaching and handling situations like these in your professional practice. This effort began in 2003, when I (Terry) edited a special issue of *Social Work & Christianity* introducing the case method of teaching with five decision cases for the Christian social work community. This book provides revised versions of those cases and additional cases which deal with other aspects of religion, spirituality, and faith in social work practice.

The cases are all decision cases, a particular type of case designed for the case method of learning. The case method of learning typically involves in-depth class discussions based on open-ended, detailed accounts of actual practice situations. These accounts require you to first formulate or decide about the problem and then to decide on a course of action. In-depth discussion of the cases will help you learn to apply theory to practice and to develop important problem solving and critical-thinking skills for professional practice.

Adapted in part from Wolfer, T. A. (2003). Decision cases for Christians in social work: Introduction to the special issue. *Social Work & Christianity, 30*(2), 103-116.

This introduction will 1) briefly describe how these cases differ from other types of cases you may have used in the classroom setting, 2) outline a rationale for using them in your learning, 3) provide background on the case writing process, 4) suggest how to read the cases, and 5) briefly describe the case method of learning and how you should approach case discussions. This information will help explain what may be an unconventional classroom experience for you once you begin reading and discussing the cases.

Distinguishing Decision Cases

What's different about these cases? There are many types of cases, ranging from brief, hypothetical vignettes to book-length, historical accounts of complex situations (Evans & Evans, 2002). However, decision cases represent a particular kind of case: "These concise cases tell the story of an actual, unresolved, problematic situation at a particular point in time. The context and events of each case are seen through the eyes of one person who is challenged to make a decision" (p. 31). Like many other kinds of cases, decision cases provide detailed accounts of social work practice situations. However, decision cases differ from most other cases in several ways.

First, perhaps most significantly, decision cases depict situations involving a dilemma of some sort for the protagonist (i.e., the social worker who reported the case) and end before the situation is resolved. As a result, decision cases stimulate readers to analyze information and define problems, and then to recommend ways to intervene in the situations.

Second, decision cases often provide more detail than traditional cases, including information about the time period, social service and other organizations, organizational and social policies, and community setting. From a systems perspective, such information often plays an essential role in considering the situation and possible solutions. But some of it is also extraneous, requiring readers to sort through the data, just as they must do in professional practice.

Third, decision cases typically include more information about the protagonists than traditional social work cases. This is important in decision cases because such information is an essential part of understanding the case and exploring the situation and possible solutions. Whereas social work cases often invite readers to identify with a generic social worker in the case (i.e., "Ms. Green"), decision cases provide details about the social worker that may be relevant for case dynamics. Putting this information on the page helps you to consider how it may influence problems and their possible resolutions. Further, this information may encourage you to consider how your own characteristics may influence your practice.

Fourth, as depictions of actual practice situations, decision cases usually do not include much theoretical content, except when it's explicitly mentioned by the case reporter. In professional practice, most situations do not present with theoretical concepts; problems have no theoretical labels attached. It's up to the practitioner to decide what theoretical concepts apply. Just as in practice, the limited theoretical content requires that you supply theory for understanding the situations, and helps you recognize the benefit of doing so. It also allows your instructor considerable latitude in discussing cases from different theoretical perspectives.

A Rationale for Learning with Decision Cases

Why use such cases in the classroom? As several authors suggest, decision cases represent an abstraction of traditional apprenticeships in the sense that they bring actual cases from the field into the classroom for students to consider together (Boehrer & Linsky, 1990; Fisher, 1978). As a result, cases provide a bridge between your class work and your field placement.

Case method learning, based on use of decision cases, is frequently advocated as a means for promoting problem solving and critical thinking skills. Authors making this claim come from professions as diverse as business, teacher education, engineering, social work and theological education (e.g., Barnes, Christensen, & Hansen, 1994; Boehrer & Linsky, 1990; Christensen, Garvin, & Sweet, 1991; Cossom, 1991; Evans & Evans, 2002; Fisher, 1978; Lundeberg, Levin & Harrington, 1999; Meyer & Jones, 1993; Prince, 2004; Prince & Felder, 2006). By providing challenging situations in which you must apply knowledge and exercise judgment, these cases help prepare you for professional practice. Decision cases require that you use your analytic and critical thinking skills, your knowledge of social work theory and research, and your common sense and collective wisdom to identify and analyze problems, to evaluate possible solutions, and to formulate a preferred intervention (Welsh & Wolfer, 2000).

Writing as business educators, Barnes, Christensen, and Hansen (1994) argue that case method instruction helps to develop in students an applied, "administrative point of view" (p. 50), what we in social work might refer to as "thinking like a social worker." They suggest that an administrative or practitioner point of view includes: 1) a focus on understanding the specific context; 2) a sense for appropriate boundaries; 3) sensitivity to interrelationships; 4) examining and understanding any situation from a multidimensional point of view; 5) accepting personal responsibility for the solution of organizational problem; and 6) an action orientation (p. 50-51).

Furthermore, an action orientation includes: a) a sense for the possible; b) willingness to make decisions on the basis of imperfect and limited data; c) a sense for the critical; d) the ability to combine discipline and creativity; e) skill in converting targets into accomplishments; and f) an appreciation of the major limits of professional action (p. 51). In short, the concept of an administrative or practitioner point of view redirects the instructor's attention from what students know to their ability to use their knowledge. From this perspective, theoretical knowledge is essential but insufficient for competent professional practice. Not only must social workers have knowledge, they must know how to use it.

As we have also argued elsewhere, the case method of learning may be particularly well suited for addressing religion and spirituality in professional practice (Sherwood, Wolfer, & Scales, 2002). Decision cases reveal the complex interplay of religious and spiritual issues in practice situations, and help to identity and illuminate the dilemmas that may result from these and other factors. Often these issues are internal to the practitioners themselves, while also present in the external environment. Compared with personal experience, however, decision cases provide a relatively less threatening forum for reflecting upon and discussing these issues.

Writing the Cases

Where did these cases come from? At the outset of this case writing project, I suggested to prospective case writers that situations appropriate for inclusion in the NACSW case collection would have several characteristics:

- First, the situation may be drawn from direct practice with individuals, families or groups or indirect practice with organizations or communities. It may be drawn from any field of social work practice.
- Second, there must be a Christian social worker interested and willing to report the situation in confidential interviews with a case writer. This individual is the case reporter.

- Third, that social worker must have decision-making responsibility in the situation reported, otherwise there would be less need for you to struggle with the dilemma.
- Finally, the situation must involve some type of dilemma for the social worker that involves faith, religion, or spirituality. For example, the dilemma may include conflicting values or ethical principles held by individual clients, their families, the social worker, the social work organization, or social policies. In the best cases, competent and sincere Christian social workers may disagree about appropriate responses to the dilemma.

As implied by these instructions, the cases were all field researched. That is, they were all based on confidential in-depth interviews with social workers who agreed to report their experiences.

Whatever you think of particular decision cases, avoid jumping to quick conclusions about the social worker, the client, and other components of the case. The case reporters have been generous and courageous in telling about particularly challenging, even troubling situations they have faced in professional practice. For that, we are most grateful. For some case reporters, the situations continue to frustrate, perplex and concern them, and that was part of the reason they agreed to report. Remember, if a protagonist was simply unethical or incompetent, the case will hold little interest and provide little challenge. In contrast, good decision cases often spark significant disagreement, even among competent and ethical practitioners, regarding the nature of the problem and how to resolve it.

Reading the Decision Cases

How should you approach these cases? These decision cases can be read on several levels. On one level, they simply depict a variety of settings that employ Christians in social work and the types of situations that occasionally crop up. Obviously, the cases represent only a small sample of social work practice fields (e.g., housing, congregations, mental health, domestic violence, public education, international development) and include both faith-based and public settings.

On a second level, the cases depict specific challenges that individual social workers encountered in particular settings and at particular points in time. From a systems perspective, the multiple and overlapping factors will be quite evident, though the specifics vary from case to case. In various combinations, these include client needs and values; social worker needs, values and skills; needs and values of other individuals related to the client(s); organizational philosophies, policies and procedures; professional social work values and ethics; government policies and laws; and Biblical, theological, and philosophical perspectives. These multiple factors create the complex and particular environments in which social workers must function, and which they must carefully consider when attempting to resolve the dilemmas.

More specifically, these cases each include a unique set of overlapping issues related to spirituality, religion, or faith on the part of clients, social workers, organizations, or communities. Go looking for that, and you will see it in many ways. Those matters of spirituality, religion, or faith seldom "trump" other issues in the cases, and do not lead to simple resolution of case dilemmas. On the contrary, considering these issues will often make situations more complex and difficult. But including these issues, where appropriate, may lead to better integration of faith and practice. In sum, efforts to honor both faith-related and professional values may create certain challenges but may also yield more competent practice.

Finally, on a third, more abstract level, the cases also reflect common challenges of social work practice across settings (and, we might add, of human experience). These include, for example, balancing client and organizational needs, resolving contradictory policy requirements, making decisions with incomplete information, identifying appropriate limits of professional intervention, anticipating unintended consequences of decisions, and resolving value or ethical dilemmas.

Learning with Decision Cases

How will you discuss these cases in your classroom? To maximize the learning potential of decision cases, your instructor will use a "case method teaching" approach. This means your instructor will primarily lead discussions by asking questions (Boehrer & Linsky, 1990; Lynn, 1999). The underlying questions for every case are: 1) What is the problem? and 2) What would you do about it?

In the actual classroom discussion, of course, your instructor will typically ask dozens of questions, and these are selected and formulated based on the instructor's goals, what background knowledge you bring to the discussion, and the direction and flow of the immediate discussion. As case discussions unfold, instructors may encourage you to elaborate on your perspectives, challenge you to justify your position, seek divergent viewpoints, and point out connections or discrepancies with comments made by your classmates. They will generally refrain from providing their own opinions. Instructors may seek to distribute speaking turns, steering the discussion away from talkative students and toward quieter students. More than other teaching approaches, case method teaching requires that instructors listen well and help you to listen well.

To benefit most from a case discussion, it's important that you both take a stand and remain open to changing your mind (Wolfer & Scales, 2006). This requires that you draw conclusions based on evidence in the case, while also recognizing that your classmates may, for example, notice things that you overlooked or interpret them differently than you, draw from their personal experience, or have background knowledge about the field of practice that informs their responses. Of course, if everyone takes a stand, as they should, this will often produce vigorous disagreements. You may feel uncomfortable taking a stand, especially in the face of such disagreements. If you have a strong desire to please or get along, you may be inclined to downplay differences in your analysis or recommendations to reduce the interpersonal tension. But this undermines the learning potential, both for you and for the entire class. Without vigorous debate, the class may not consider diverse perspectives and may miss opportunities to practice articulating and supporting their ideas. This is good experience for professional practice because social workers must often work with people who disagree (e.g., families, boards of directors, interdisciplinary groups, congregations). Case discussions can help you learn to do so in direct and respectful ways.

In summary, we think that grappling with these cases will help you develop and refine your abilities for analyzing and resolving difficult situations. And we think that grappling with these cases will help you develop increasing competence, from both professional and Christian perspectives.

To the Instructor

For the decision cases in this collection, case authors have written extensive teaching notes (TNs). The TNs have several components to help instructors make thorough and efficient use of the cases. To help instructors choose among the cases, the notes include a brief case synopsis, a BSW- or MSW-level designation, and possible learning outcomes. To help instructors lead a case discussion, the notes include possible discussion questions and responses, additional teaching suggestions (i.e., activities to supplement the case discussion), and background readings for instructors or students (e.g., books, journal articles, web sites). Following a common pattern in case method teaching, the TNs organize the possible discussion questions into four categories:

- Facts: to clarify factual information in the case that may be unfamiliar or confusing for students at the outset of the case discussion.
- Analysis: to illuminate the basic dimensions and often controversial issues in the case, to encourage students to think critically and across system levels, and ultimately to define the problem.
- Practice: to consider costs and benefits, intended and unintended consequences, and ethical implications of various courses of action, and to develop and recommend a specific course of action.
- Reflection: to encourage students to explore their personal reactions to aspects of a case or personal qualities that may affect their professional "use of self."

However, the teaching notes do not contain "answers" to the cases or tell how things "turned out." Even so, the TNs are reserved for instructors only to preserve the full challenge for students of understanding and resolving the case dilemmas. Instructors can download the TNs from the educator section of the NACSW web site.

References

Barnes, L. B., Christensen, C. R., & Hansen, A. J. (1994). *Teaching and the case method* (3rd ed.). Boston: Harvard Business School Press.

Boehrer, J., & Linsky, M. (1990). Teaching with cases: Learning to question. In M. D. Svinicki (Ed.), *The changing face of college teaching* (pp. 41-57). San Francisco: Jossey-Bass.

Christensen, C. R., Garvin, D. A., & Sweet, A. (Eds.). (1991). *Education for judgment: The artistry of discussion leadership*. Boston: Harvard Business School Press.

Cossom, J. (1991). Teaching from cases: Education for critical thinking. *Journal of Teaching in Social Work, 5*, 139-155.

Evans, A. F., & Evans, R. A. (2002). Using case studies in urban theological education. In E. Villafañe, B. W. Jackson, R. A. Evans, & A. F. Evans (Eds.), *Transforming the city: Reframing education for urban ministry* (pp. 30-35). Grand Rapids, MI: William B. Eerdmans Publishing.

Fisher, C. F. (1978). Being there vicariously by case studies. In M. Ohmer and Associates (Ed.), *On college teaching: A guide to contemporary practices* (pp. 258-285). San Francisco: Jossey-Bass.

Lundeberg, M. A., Levin, B. B., & Harrington, H. L. (1999). *Who learns what from cases and how? The research base for teaching with cases.* Mahwah, NJ: Lawrence Erlbaum.

Lynn, L. E., Jr. (1999). *Teaching and learning with cases: A guidebook.* New York: Chatham House.

Meyer C., & Jones, T. B. (1993). Case studies. *Promoting active learning: Strategies for the college classroom* (pp. 103-119). San Francisco: Jossey-Bass.

Prince, M. J. (2004). Does active learning work? A review of the research. *Journal of Engineering Education, 93*(3), 223-231.

Prince, M. J., & Felder, R. M. (2006). Inductive teaching and learning methods: Definitions, comparisons and research bases. *Journal of Engineering Education, 95*(2), 123-138.

Sherwood, D. A., Wolfer, T. A., & Scales, T. L. (2002). Introduction: Spirituality and religion, decision cases, and competent social work practice. In T. L. Scales, T. A. Wolfer, D. A. Sherwood, D. R. Garland, B. Hugen, & S. W. Pittman (Eds.), *Spirituality and religion in social work practice: Decision cases with teaching notes* (pp. 1- 10). Alexandria, VA: Council on Social Work Education.

Welsh, M. F., & Wolfer, T. A. (2000, February). *Making a case for case method teaching in social work education.* Faculty Development Institute presented at the Annual Program Meeting of the Council on Social Work Education, New York, NY.

Wolfer, T. A., & Scales, T. L. (2006). Tips for learning from decision cases. In T. A. Wolfer & T. L. Scales (Eds.), *Decision cases for advanced social work practice: Thinking like a social worker* (pp. 17-25). Belmont, CA: Thomson Brooks/Cole.

1

SISTER'S KEEPER

Christine Kessen

"Don't tell!" 17-year-old Debbie Richards shouted as her substance abuse counselor, Rickie Norris, got up to leave the office. Tears streamed down Debbie's face.

Rickie felt herself weakening. It was mid-October 2002, and she had been working with Debbie since September, 2001, shortly after beginning work as an Assessment Specialist at Cuyahoga County Department of Justice Affairs providing aftercare services for juvenile offenders. She knew well the many traumas in Debbie's troubled life and didn't want to contribute more stress. *But isn't this too dangerous?* she wondered with alarm. *Known drug dealers in the home again. No adult supervision.*

"They'll take my sister away," Debbie sobbed.

Rickie struggled with her own feelings of disgust. She remembered the past physical abuse and current neglect which Debbie and her sister endured. *The sheer irresponsibility of that mother!* Rickie fumed. Calming herself, she tried to offer Debbie what small comfort she could before leaving the room to look for help.

Cuyahoga County (Ohio) Department of Justice Affairs, Division of Treatment Services

Cuyahoga County (Ohio) government established the Division of Treatment Services and the Youth Development Center (juvenile detention facility) within the county's Department of Justice Affairs to accomplish its stated mission of prevent-

Development of this decision case was supported in part by the University of South Carolina College of Social Work. It was prepared solely to provide material for class discussion and not to suggest either effective or ineffective handling of the situation depicted. While based on field research regarding an actual situation, names and certain facts may have been disguised to protect confidentiality. The author and editors wish to thank the anonymous case reporter for cooperation in making this account available for the benefit of social work students and practitioners.

ing juvenile delinquency, protecting public safety, and providing opportunities for adjudicated youth to learn responsible behavior in a safe, protective environment. The Division was charged with providing aftercare services for juvenile offenders released from the Youth Development Center. Lasting from three months to two years, aftercare services included time-limited substance abuse groups as well as individual and family treatment. As a county-funded agency, the Division was always short of cash and workers. However, all twenty direct service workers were professionally trained, including the eight case managers.

The professional staff were concerned about the old, dingy office building housing the Division of Treatment Services in downtown Cleveland. The standard off-white paint was peeling from the walls. Juveniles encountered adult offenders who came to the same building for counseling. The staff did what they could to add cheer to the place. For example, they ordered colorful upholstered chairs and put up scenic posters on the walls. One worker attached a magnet of her dog Oscar to an otherwise drab gray metal desk. The committed staff wanted to say "you matter" to the youth and families who visited them.

Trudy Atherton, BSW, LSW

Trudy Atherton had worked as a case manager at the Division of Treatment Services for the past two and one half years and as a Child and Family Service (CFS) case investigator for three years previously. While comparatively young at age twenty-seven, she had the needed expertise. Skilled at the organizational tasks of case management, Trudy enjoyed her daily conversations with other professionals. "I always learn something," she told Rickie. Having graduated with a bachelor's degree in social work five years before, Trudy frequently discussed her plans to complete her master's degree. "Now I'm not sure," she told Rickie over lunch.

Married for less than a year, Trudy looked forward to spending her evenings with her husband fixing up their new home. She began to notice how difficult it was to leave the office on time in the evening. "While I enjoy case management," she confided to Rickie, "I need time for my own life!"

Despite these personal concerns, Trudy welcomed the opportunity to work with Debbie. "With a little effort," she told Rickie, "we can set this girl on the right track." As required by agency protocol, Trudy developed a case plan addressing all of Debbie's known problems and reviewed the plan with her supervisor weekly.

Rickie Norris, MSSA, LSW

At age thirty-five, Rickie could only guess at the experiences that Debbie reported. Raised in a caring Christian family in suburban Erie, Pennsylvania, Rickie accepted Christ as her Savior when she was nine and remained active in her church.

Rickie enjoyed staying in her home community after graduating from high school. She attended college part time and paid her tuition through office work. Earning a bachelors degree in communications with a minor in psychology, Rickie worked in business for two years. "I was saved but not always walking with God," she would honestly report. "Baptized as an adult in 1998, I rededicated my life to Christ which led me to social work."

Entering the graduate social work program at Case Western Reserve University, Rickie decided to concentrate in alcohol and drug abuse studies. Having experienced first-hand the family problems associated with the substance abuse of several uncles, she felt called to help others. As part of her studies, Rickie interned, first, with the Division of Treatment Services and, then, with a substance abuse treatment program at a Veterans Administration hospital.

Graduating in May, 2001, Rickie immediately put her substance abuse training to work as an Assessment Specialist in the Division of Treatment Services of the County Department of Justice Affairs. Rickie excelled and was promoted to Substance Abuse Program Coordinator within her first year. In addition to her administrative tasks, Rickie was the primary worker for 15 - 20 juvenile clients. She conducted two weekly substance abuse groups and provided individual counseling for one to five clients. But at the end of the day, Rickie could not leave her work at the office.

For Rickie, social work was a Christian vocation. She thought of Jesus as the *ultimate* social worker. When uncertain how to proceed with a difficult case, Rickie often sought His guidance by asking herself, "What would Jesus do?" She bristled at the limitations of working in a government agency. Although she prayed regularly for her clients, Rickie knew that she could not freely discuss her belief in Christ and the saving grace of Jesus with them. She was beginning to consider the idea of working for a faith-based organization where she could practice her faith more openly. Rickie looked to her Bible Study and singles groups at the Grace Christian and Missionary Alliance Church in suburban Cleveland for support and challenge as she struggled with this decision.

Rickie's faith continued to sustain her through the low points in her work with addicted adolescents. She felt a special connection with Debbie who professed to be a struggling Christian. *Could there be ways to share one's faith with a Christian client?* Rickie wondered.

Rickie first met Debbie right after her release from the juvenile detention center when Trudy referred her for outpatient group treatment. With six girls participating, Rickie's group focused on education about substance abuse and relapse prevention. Rickie observed that Debbie appeared eager to please and to succeed with her program. Her first treatment notes were encouraging -- "Debbie participates well in group treatment" and "Debbie is insightful about her substance abuse issues." Four or five months later, however, she recorded "Debbie came to the office high on drugs" and "Grandmother called concerned that Debbie is skipping school and not returning home at night." Consulting with Trudy, Rickie obtained authorization to provide individual treatment for Debbie. Rickie hoped that the one-on-one support would help Debbie regain her sobriety.

Debbie Richards

As described in the Division of Treatment Services case records, Debbie Richards was a tall, thin, attractive seventeen-year-old African American woman. Debbie's good looks and upbeat manner, however, belied her true physical and emotional state. Diagnosed with severe substance abuse, Debbie recalled using drugs as long as she could remember. As a child, she often found alcohol and marijuana lying around the house. Her mother was usually too "out of it" to notice if she used any. Now Debbie was addicted to "wet," the street name for a form of PCP (phencyclidine). Debbie and her friends smoked cigarettes dipped in "wet" for the thrill of the resulting hallucinations.

CFS first learned about Debbie when she was four years old. While her mother was away, a live-in boyfriend molested her following a violent rampage in which he had knifed and killed the family dog and her newborn puppies. After the incident, a relative found Debbie hiding in the basement and called the police.

The court awarded custody of Debbie to her maternal grandmother who had cared for her during previous crises. When Debbie was in her grandmother's care, she regularly attended school where she excelled in English and writing. Her grandmother served her nourishing meals, took her to the local Baptist church on Sundays, and supervised her friends and activities. Debbie occasionally visited her father although their relationship was never close. (Previously, her mother had not allowed such visits because she and Debbie's father had never married.) CFS reported that the grandmother provided a stable home and appropriate supervision for Debbie. However, Debbie missed her mother and periodically returned to visit her in a part of town known for having drug dealers on every corner. Although able to maintain sobriety at her grandmother's home, Debbie would relapse when visiting her mother.

In an effort at family reunification, the courts returned thirteen-year-old Debbie to the home of her mother, Sandra Richards. Sandra had remained a bright and capable woman at thirty-seven. A high school graduate, she had completed some college courses. Now, however, she was working as a factory worker due to her frequent bouts with alcoholism and heavy gambling. Never married, she struggled to support herself and her two daughters.

Debbie's relationship with her mother remained somewhat distant despite the change in custody. Sandra often required Debbie to baby-sit for her younger sister, Cheryl, while Sandra drank and entertained men friends in the home. Afraid of the drug dealers and other men visiting her mother, Debbie would sometimes leave the house, and leave Cheryl unattended.

Debbie's own drug abuse and delinquent behavior accelerated after her return to her mother's home. When Debbie turned fourteen, Sandra filed charges against her for unruly behavior (truancy, violating curfew). Initially sentencing Debbie to probation, the court later convicted her for violating probation, citing missed appointments with her probation officer and "dirty urines." When confronted in court, Debbie admitted using marijuana, alcohol, and "wet." The judge sentenced Debbie at age sixteen to the Youth Development Center (YDC) where she stayed for seven months.

After her release from YDC, the court ordered Debbie to the Division of Treatment Services for aftercare with Trudy Atherton. Trudy's initial assessment for the court described Debbie as "highly motivated" and "accepting of treatment." In addition to case management, Debbie attended ten weeks of outpatient substance abuse group treatment with Rickie as group leader. After the group ended, Debbie occasionally stopped by the Division office to say "hi" to Rickie. After a relapse, she began individual treatment with Rickie. She attended the first four sessions but then missed many appointments. Still, Debbie kept in contact with Rickie for several months. On her last return to treatment, Debbie explained that she had started using drugs again at her mother's home. Strung out on "wet," she had called her aunt to pick her up and take her back to her grandmother. Debbie told Rickie that she was determined to stay sober.

New problems: Friday's treatment session

Arriving on time for a second session after her latest relapse, Debbie appeared distracted and preoccupied. "I need to leave early today to pick up Cheryl at school," she announced to Rickie. With little prodding, Debbie explained that she dreaded returning to her mother's home but felt responsible for her sister's safety after school.

"Cheryl needs me to fix her a sandwich," Debbie said, "I help her with her homework and get her clothes ready for school. I can't count on Mom. Lately she's more concerned with Derek—that jerk is always bringing her dope."

After pressing for more information, Rickie mentioned that she might need to report the case to CFS for Cheryl's protection.

Debbie immediately protested. "I can take care of my sister," she shouted. "You'll make things worse!"

Not surprised by Debbie's strong reaction, Rickie also worried about the consequences if she reported the case to the state child protective services agency. *Would I be helping or causing more harm?* she wondered. *With apparent neglect but no current abuse, would CFS do anything anyway?* Rickie remembered when Sandra threw out all of Debbie's clothes after Debbie decided to stay with her grandmother - *what vengeful actions might my reporting provoke?*

What this child has lived through! Rickie remembered. *On and off drugs! Pulled out of a stable home! It's heartbreaking—truly a case of children suffering from the sins of the parents.*

Parting from Debbie, Rickie prayed that Debbie's faith would sustain her through this latest crisis. *Jesus, put a ring of protection around her; soften her heart toward You. Put someone in her path that will bring her closer to You.* She thought of the people who regularly crossed Debbie's path and how they pulled her further away from God. *Am I the person God is putting in Debbie's life?* Rickie wondered. *I feel the moral obligation to be wise, but I don't feel very wise this afternoon. I feel the weight of this responsibility. Should I report or not?*

Emergency case conference

Rickie immediately consulted the agency policy and procedure manual for guidance. She found no agency protocol regarding reporting cases of neglect. *I guess we're on our own,* she thought.

Next, Rickie began looking for Trudy. She appreciated having someone with Trudy's experience on the case. *Trudy is not territorial like some case managers,* she thought. *I'm glad that we have a good working relationship.* She glanced at the clock on the wall - already 3 p.m. On a beautiful autumn afternoon, Rickie wondered whether Trudy would still be at the office. *Why do crises always happen late in the day?*

Rickie was relieved to find Trudy returning to her office after a home visit. As case manager, Trudy would make the agency's final decision about reporting. *Yet I know that I am also responsible,* Rickie thought. *As a professional social worker, I have a legal mandate to report my suspicions. Ethically I want to do whatever is best for Debbie and Cheryl. But how do I know what's best?* Both Trudy and Rickie reviewed their cases regularly with their clinical supervisors but neither supervisor was available in this emergency.

Rickie shared the new information about Debbie's situation with Trudy. "Everything is getting progressively worse," Rickie explained. "Debbie is reporting that her mother is inviting drug dealers into the home again. In that environment, it's almost impossible for Debbie not to use drugs again herself. She tries leaving the house but then she worries about her little sister - there's no one else to watch her. Debbie looks a real mess today. Her hair is greasy, which you know is not like her. She told me that there is no hot water in the home and that she has to bathe with water heated in a hot pot. The gas has been shut off for months and it doesn't look like her mother is doing anything about it."

"Sounds serious," Trudy confirmed.

"Do you remember Debbie's mother?" Rickie asked. "We made a home visit a few months ago when we needed her consent for Debbie's treatment plan."

"A good talker," Trudy recalled. "I had the feeling that she was putting on a good act."

"I was disgusted with her," Rickie responded. "Sandra acting like nothing was wrong! The condition of those children! I had to hold myself 'in check' the entire interview."

"I tried to help by offering her substance abuse treatment," Trudy recalled, "but she refused, insisting there was nothing wrong with her drinking."

"Well, the drinking and drugging are just getting worse," Rickie responded.

"What do you think will help now?" Trudy asked.

"I'd like to report it," Rickie said, "but you know how CFS is about neglect cases. Sometimes I wonder why we even bother. Remember the Mathews case? And the Sullivan case? CFS didn't even investigate. So much depends on which worker happens to get the call. Debbie's little sister is physically safe, but won't she be traumatized and damaged by that environment?"

"I agree with you," Trudy replied, "but neglect that isn't life-threatening is not that important to CFS when they have so many cases of serious physical abuse. Often CFS will just screen out a neglect case without investigation."

"And if we do report it and they do nothing," Rickie continued, "I worry that Debbie's mother will be vindictive again. With all her drugging, I hate to think what she could do to hurt Debbie."

"With the gas shut off and winter not far away, I think we're more likely to get action on this case than others we've reported," Trudy said. "CFS would have to go out to the home. I'm not sure what they would do once they investigated, but I know their procedures and they would have to open a case."

"That would also concern me," Rickie said. "Then I would worry about Debbie being cut off from her sister. Debbie is very upset. She was sobbing in my office, begging me not to tell. She fears that CFS will place Cheryl in foster care and that she will hardly ever get to see her. Can you think of a place where Debbie and Cheryl can stay together?" asked Rickie.

"I can't think of anyone in the family that I haven't tried already," Trudy replied.

"Didn't her aunt take Debbie in recently?" Rickie asked.

"Yes," Trudy replied, "but her aunt has four children of her own and can only manage Debbie for a night or two. She's great in a crisis, really cares about Debbie, but her resources are limited. Besides, she thinks Debbie does well at her grandmother's."

"I do, too," Rickie agreed, "but she's in her 70s and I don't think she could manage a small child, even with Debbie's help."

"Have you thought about what it would do to your relationship with Debbie if we report the case?" Trudy asked. The expression on Trudy's face showed concern. She knew how much Debbie meant to Rickie.

"I'm not worried about Debbie's reaction," Rickie replied. "After all, Debbie's perspective is skewed. A good part of the time she's strung out on PCP. My heart goes out to her, but my concern is for her best welfare. We're the professionals with experience. I just want the outcome to be the best care possible for both Debbie and Cheryl."

"Well, what would you like to see happen?" Trudy asked.

"I'd like to see the little girl adopted into a loving Christian family," Rickie said, "but I don't know if reporting the neglect will make that happen - you know she is often unsupervised."

"Parental rights would have to be terminated," Trudy commented. "Unlikely."

"Kids are so helpless," Rickie protested. "As adults we have some control over our environment, but children have none."

"One more question," Trudy added. "Do you believe that Debbie is telling you the truth? She's lied to you before," Trudy reminded.

"Yes," Rickie replied, "but that was about her drug usage. About everything else, her story has always turned out to be correct. I think she's telling the truth about this situation. You should have seen her crying about her sister."

"I asked because CFS may not believe an adolescent if there is no other substantiation," Trudy said, "although they'd still investigate."

In the course of their conversation, Rickie realized her concern for Debbie's soul. *Debbie and her grandmother are part of the body of Christ*, she thought. *Don't I have some responsibility as a fellow Christian?* Rickie also realized that she didn't know whether Trudy had religious beliefs. She wasn't sure that it would be appropriate to ask.

Trudy brought Rickie back to the task at hand by motioning toward the phone. "If we do report," Trudy said, "we should move on it now."

I know the law says to report even if it does no good, Rickie thought, *but I could be making the situation worse. Debbie and Cheryl might be split up. Sandra could really hurt them. I really want to do what's best for these children.*

2

The Grace House Ministry (A)

Michael E. Sherr & Terry A. Wolfer

Randy Samuels, a licensed clinical social worker, moved to Gastonia, North Carolina, in March of 2000, after accepting a position at the Mecklenburg County Mental Health Center. Randy and his family were at a park in their new neighborhood when they met a couple who invited them to visit Grace Presbyterian Church. They accepted the invitation and started attending regularly. A few months later, an elder from the church called Randy to ask if he would be willing to meet with a family that came to the church for help. When he agreed, he never imagined he would become so involved in the church's outreach ministry. What began as a one-time event, though, turned into a weekly commitment.

As he invested more time helping the church leaders, he came to believe that the church could be more effective in helping families if they changed how they utilized their resources. After talking to the pastor, Randy was invited to discuss his concerns with other church leaders. During the meeting, Eric Young, one of the church elders, asked, "What do you suggest we do?" As the church elders looked on expectantly, Randy pondered how to respond. He had a few suggestions but wasn't sure which ones to share.

Development of this decision case was supported in part by the University of South Carolina College of Social Work. It was prepared solely to provide material for class discussion and not to suggest either effective or ineffective handling of the situation depicted. While based on field research regarding an actual situation, names and certain facts may have been disguised to protect confidentiality. The authors and editors wish to thank the anonymous case reporter for cooperation in making this account available for the benefit of social work students and practitioners.

Revised from Sherr, M. E., & Wolfer, T. A. (2003). The Grace House Ministry (A). *Social Work & Christianity, 30*(2), 142-148. Copyright © 2003 NACSW.

Grace Presbyterian Church

Grace Presbyterian Church was a member of the Presbyterian Church in America (PCA), a conservative denomination that historically focused more on evangelism than on social ministry. The congregation was only six years old. It began as a church plant to reach people in the town of Gastonia, a suburb of Charlotte, North Carolina. Six members from Redeemer Presbyterian Church, a large PCA congregation in Charlotte, began meeting at the home of Steve Edwards, who eventually became the new congregation's first pastor. As the membership grew, the church started meeting on Sundays in the fellowship hall of a Seventh Day Adventist church. On Christmas Eve of 2001, the church moved into its own building located in an upper middle-class neighborhood. There were currently 200-250 members at Grace. The majority of the church was young, and no one at the church was over the age of 62.

As in any other PCA congregation, the leadership of Grace Presbyterian Church consisted of a core group of elders. The elders were in charge of ensuring that the church maintained its focus on the gospel of Jesus Christ. The elders were also responsible for the daily operations and finances of the church. Only elders had an official vote on the direction of the church. The pastor, associate pastor, and youth minister were all elders. There were deacons who were in charge of carrying out all social outreach ministries, including managing the deacon fund, meeting with church members and other people in the community who needed assistance, and leading the small prayer groups. Once a month, every elder and deacon would meet to discuss church business. The meetings were an official gathering called the Session. Only men could serve as elders or deacons in the PCA denomination.

Randy Samuels

At age 27, Randy Samuels graduated from the MSW program at East Carolina University. He did his advanced year field placement at Pitt County Mental Health Center and was hired full-time in the same position after graduation. As a psychiatric social worker in a partial hospitalization program, Randy developed and facilitated five hours of mental health groups each day. He also performed psychosocial and substance abuse evaluations with new clients, and crisis intervention work with the emergency services unit every third weekend. He stayed at Pitt County Mental Health Center for two years until he completed all of his requirements to be licensed in North Carolina as a clinical social worker (LCSW). He then accepted a position as the lead therapist on an intensive family and child unit at Mecklenburg County Mental Health Center. He and his family bought a house in Gastonia, where he was living with his wife and two children.

In April 2000, Randy Samuels and his family started attending Grace Presbyterian Church. They found the congregation very welcoming and were invited to participate in several different worship activities. Within a few weeks, his family was participating in weekly small prayer groups, Randy was going to the men's early-morning prayer time, and his wife and children joined the mother's morning out program. In June 2000, after completing the new membership class and being examined by the elders, Randy and his family became members of Grace Presbyterian Church.

Getting Involved

For several months everything was going smoothly. He and his family were getting adjusted to their new home, Randy was enjoying his work, and they were fully connected to the church. In the process of getting to know other church members, members asked Randy about his occupation. He explained that he was a licensed clinical social worker employed at the Mecklenburg County Mental Health Center.

Up to this point, Randy's involvement at the church was limited to participating in the usual church activities. No one asked him to help out with any of the church functions, nor did he volunteer to serve in any capacity. He was comfortable with how church fit into his life. He used to think to himself, "I'm a social worker; I participate in social ministry each and every day. I don't need to do more on my own time."

Then one evening around 9:00 o'clock, Kenneth Baum, a church elder, called the Samuel's house to speak with Randy.

Randy's wife, Lynn, answered the phone. "Hello?"

"Hi, Lynn, this is Kenneth Baum from Grace."

"Oh, hi, Kenneth."

"Lynn, I was wondering if I could speak with Randy for a minute."

"Sure, I'll go get him."

After a few moments Randy picked up the phone. "Hey, Kenneth, how are you, brother?"

"I'm fine, Randy. I am sorry to bother you so late in the evening."

"That's okay, what can I do for you?"

"Randy, the pastor thought you might be able to help us with something."

"Sure, what is it?"

"Well, you see, a woman came to the church this morning asking for help. Apparently she and her two children have been living out of their car for the past few weeks. We put them up at a local motel for the weekend, but we're not sure what to do next. Randy, the pastor and I were wondering if you would be willing to meet with the woman after church on Sunday. We told her that you were a social worker and she was willing to talk with you."

"Sure, I don't know how much help I will be, but I can at least help you figure out what to do next."

"Great, I'll tell Pastor Edwards and we'll schedule a meeting right after service on Sunday."

"Okay, I'll see you then."

When Randy hung up the phone Lynn asked, "What did Kenneth want?"

"They want me to meet with a woman they're trying to help."

"Oh, I think that's great."

"Yeah, I don't mind helping out, I just don't want to get too involved."

"Well, it's only one meeting; besides, I think it will be good for you to help out."

That Sunday, Randy met with Kenneth, Pastor Steve Edwards, and the woman. Within an hour Randy helped the woman identify and prioritize her needs, and facilitated a discussion between Kenneth, the pastor, and the woman to determine specific steps the church could take to help. After the meeting the pastor shared with Randy how impressed he was with how Randy handled the whole situation.

Is There a Better Way?

Over the next few weeks the pastor and other church leaders began asking Randy to help more frequently. As he continued to volunteer his time to meet with families, he was beginning to observe some problems in the church's helping process. One evening after meeting with another family, Randy and the pastor were walking out to their cars when Randy asked,

"Steve, can I talk with you for a minute?"

"Sure, Randy."

"Steve, I have some concerns about how the church uses the deacon fund. I think it's great that Grace wants to be a place that people in need feel welcome. And I am honored that you and the elders want me to help. But, it seems to me the church gives out money from the deacon fund too sporadically. It also seems that Grace is trying to do everything for everyone."

"Well, Randy, the deacon fund is the church's main source of outreach ministry. We use it to help families in a way that may lead them to being receptive to hearing the Gospel. It's meant to be used for such purposes and we don't want to be stingy."

"I understand what you're saying, Steve. But lately, every time the church tries to help, the church discovers that the needs of these families are more complex then they initially appear. In my opinion the type of help the church provides is basically a temporary band-aid to deal with a symptom of a greater problem."

"What's that?"

"Poverty. And it takes more than paying someone's utility bill or buying a week's worth of groceries to help these families get on their feet."

"Brother, tell me about it. Sometimes we get frustrated and feel helpless. But I'll tell you, Randy, Grace is a church for the nonbeliever and especially those in need. Besides, as I often say at the leadership meetings, I like doing something better than doing nothing."

"Steve, a fundamental principle that I learned at school, and one I experience as a social worker, is that there are always unlimited needs and limited resources. And that is why, until Christ returns, I will always have a job. As a congregation, I think it is important for Grace to think about how they can provide the most effective help, given our limited resources. Otherwise, Grace will continue to provide superficial help, without really making a difference."

"You have a point, Randy. Listen, the Session is meeting Monday, January 8th. Why don't you plan to attend so we can talk about this with the entire leadership team?"

"Okay, I'll be there."

"Great. The Session meets at 7:00 o'clock in the fellowship hall next to the staff offices."

Addressing the Session

When Randy arrived, the elders and deacons were already sitting around four tables arranged to form a large rectangle. The only open seats were at the end of the tables closest to the doorway. Randy sat down at the edge of the table next to one of the deacons. Although everyone was friendly and the atmosphere appeared informal, he felt a little insecure sitting among all of these church leaders.

Steve started the meeting by welcoming everyone to the meeting. He added, "Randy, we wanted to thank you for coming tonight."

Randy replied, "Well, I am both honored and humbled to be here. To be honest, I am a little bit nervous."

"Well, Randy, I approach each Session meeting with a reverent fear, recognizing the magnitude of our responsibility as leaders of this congregation. We spend a lot of time praying for God's will for this congregation. We also get updates from each of the small prayer group leaders and talk about many of the church's ministries and activities. Sometimes we're here past 11:00 o'clock. You'll be first on the agenda so you can get home to your family. "

Looking over to the left side of the room, the pastor looked at one of the deacons and asked, "Matt, would you open us up in prayer?"

Matt replied, "Of course," and everyone in the room bowed their heads and closed their eyes as Matt prayed. When he finished, Jeff Hatling, the deacon who managed the deacon fund, quickly turned to Randy.

"Randy, the pastor called me the other evening and filled me in on your conversation with him. Can you briefly tell the rest of the Session some of your concerns?"

Randy paused for a moment to gather his thoughts. "Well, when I started helping some of you with different families, I thought that it was great that the church even attempted to help such families. I thought to myself that Grace was a special place that really wanted to share the Gospel with everyone, no matter what his or her circumstances. But the more I became involved, the more I began to notice how the church begins a helping relationship with families, only to later find out that their issues are more complex than they initially appeared. As a result, the church sort of runs out of steam and gets frustrated helping these families. I am also concerned that Grace ends up unintentionally reinforcing a mistrust that many of these families may have for the church."

"What do you mean, Randy?" asked the pastor.

"In social work, when families have bad experiences dealing with other social workers, it makes it more difficult to establish a helping relationship with them. I can't even begin to tell you how many families I work with that are so mistrusting because of an experience they had with a therapist or social worker that ended poorly. I always have to be careful that in the process of developing a relationship with a family, I don't perpetuate the same pattern by promising too much, and not being able to deliver. In my opinion, the same holds true for the church. We don't want to offer help and refuge to families, tell them about Christ's unconditional love, only to turn them away when we realize that a family's issues may require more time and money than we originally expected."

After what seemed to Randy like a long silence, Eric Young, one of the elders turned to Randy. "You know, we would love to be able to provide the kind of help these families need, but we just don't have the resources. We also don't want to turn anyone away. What do you suggest we do?"

Randy wondered what to say. He knew that PCA churches normally don't get involved in social service programs. However, he sensed that Grace was really committed to helping people. He also remembered Steve's sermons about the church being a place of refuge for the lost and downtrodden. Randy had a few suggestions but he wasn't sure which ones to share or where to begin.

3

THE LETTER

Mackenzi Huyser & Maggie Wiles

As she prepared for an afternoon appointment, social worker Carrie Peterson reviewed the limited information she had about her new client, Siu Lee. A County health nurse had called Carrie a couple of times to learn about what services Carrie's agency, My Sister's Place, offered and mentioned she was working with a client who was in need of domestic violence services. During the last call, she asked to schedule an appointment for the client on Tuesday afternoon. Carrie asked her to have the client call, if at all possible. Later that afternoon, Siu Lee called to confirm the Tuesday appointment. The situation seemed similar to other cases Carrie had worked with before, but Carrie was intrigued as to why this particular this client had asked for a faith-based organization.

My Sister's Place

Founded in 1980 by a group of Christian women, My Sister's Place became an important source of shelter and counseling services for many who suffered from domestic violence in the Chicagoland area. My Sister's Place fulfilled a need for faith-based programming, especially for women of faith. For many of them, the agency was more acceptable than secular organizations because it focused on helping women through the lens of faith.

The agency staff included three full-time counselors with masters degrees in

Development of this decision case was supported in part by the University of South Carolina College of Social Work. It was prepared solely to provide material for class discussion and not to suggest either effective or ineffective handling of the situation depicted. While based on field research regarding an actual situation, names and certain facts may have been disguised to protect confidentiality. The authors and editors wish to thank the anonymous case reporter for cooperation in making this account available for the benefit of social work students and practitioners.

counseling, two family service providers with BSWs, and a number of direct care staff who served in the shelter program. The counselors and family service providers were assigned cases through an intake referral for families receiving services in either the shelter or non-shelter programs.

Most of the women who came for services, through either the shelter or other programs, were Christian. The agency, however, had a long history of serving women of other faiths or no faiths as well, and staff members were encouraged to attend trainings on different cultural and religious traditions. Recently, the agency had encouraged their staff members to attend training on the relation between domestic violence and various cultural or religious beliefs. Many staff members had commented that they found the training useful and informative in working with clients from different backgrounds. Overall, the agency was committed to working within a client's frame of reference.

The agency was known in the Christian faith community as a welcoming place. The agency's funding came primarily from individual donors, most of whom were Christian, and secondarily from Christian organizations and churches. The staff of My Sister's Place recognized that Christian donors often struggled to understand and appreciate the balance it sought to achieve between honoring the sacrament of marriage and women's physical and emotional safety.

Carrie Peterson

Carrie had grown up in a Christian home attending church and Sunday school each week before she headed off to college at Trinity Christian College. Carrie believed that God needed to be in the center of human relationships and that it was through the grace of God and the death of his son, Jesus Christ, that her sins were forgiven. She also believed that though she had been redeemed completely through God's grace and power, she still had a part to play in the redemption of the world. Carrie believed that all Christians are called to be a part of bringing about the new creation (because the first creation had fallen to sin) through the way that they live every part of their lives. It was her responsibility and calling to be a co-worker with Christ in working towards transforming the world and everything in it to glorify God. Once at college, however, Carrie encountered different concepts and opinions. She often found herself out of her comfort zone, challenged to think about new ideas and ways of looking at life.

Freshman philosophy courses challenged Carrie to think about her own worldview and what made her outlook on life different from people who described themselves as humanists or pantheists. She enjoyed thinking about these ideas and engaging in the class debates. Nevertheless, Carrie had limited interaction with people having worldviews different than her own. She often wondered how someone could find strength and hope in these different perspectives when to her they seemed so inadequate.

As Carrie learned more about the social work profession and the opportunities that existed, she knew this was the field she wanted to pursue. She felt the desire to meet and interact with people different than herself. Her friends always said she had a heart to help and Carrie knew this was true. The field of domestic violence was of interest to her and so when the time came to apply for field placements, she put it at the top of her list. Her professor arranged for her to interview at My Sister's Place.

Once in her field placement, however, she felt awkward dealing with issues of faith and domestic violence. She had grown up in a Christian community where no one hung out their dirty laundry and no one discussed violence in the home. Nevertheless, she had a passion and a calling to help and support the women she encountered at My Sister's Place. Carrie's love for them gave her a passion to empower the women so that they might seek better situations for themselves and their families. She believed that women experiencing domestic violence were in need and deserving of God's grace and unconditional love. As the end of her internship neared, Carrie decided she would like to pursue full-time employment at My Sister's Place and asked to be considered for one of their openings.

One day before she completed her internship, Carrie was offered and eagerly accepted the Family Advocate position at My Sister's Place. She began her new position immediately after graduation. Each day, Carrie felt challenged to learn from her clients and empower them to make life-changing decisions.

Carrie enjoyed many aspects of her position, from case management and re-ferral for services to advocating for clients and helping them gain access to new programs. But most of all she loved the look of confidence a woman acquired after she was empowered to live a life free of abuse and had started anew.

Tuesday Afternoon—Initial Appointment

Carrie had just finished putting together an information packet for Siu Lee when the receptionist announced that Siu and her children had arrived in the waiting area. Carrie suggested Siu's children could remain in the small supervised play area while she and Siu met. Siu nodded and showed her two young boys to the play area. As they walked together down the hall, Carrie noticed how timid and quiet Siu behaved. *Perhaps she's nervous*, Carrie thought. Carrie offered Siu a seat at the table in her office, and joined her with the referral form and information packet.

"Your health nurse gave me some information about your current situation," Carrie began. "Could you give me some more information about what brings you here today?"

Looking into Carrie's kind face, with little warning, Siu began to cry uncontrollably. Carrie sat, feeling uncomfortable, and looked to Siu for an explanation. Siu continued to cry for several minutes and then, just as abruptly, sat back and stopped crying. She appeared exhausted.

"I tell you my story," Siu began slowly. "My young son, Lanh, he have bad pain in ears and fever. He have this pain many times. My husband send me to nurse for him. He say, 'Take bus and go.' He put children and me on bus and tell driver what stop I get off. I very afraid. I come to nurse only by help from people I meet on bus."

Siu continued, telling of the long process to meet the health nurse who would help her and her son.

"I know not go home without see nurse, or my husband angry," Siu explained. "I tell worker I had much trouble finding building, she not care, so I afraid tell her I not speak good English. We sit in waiting room five hours. When we meet nurse I tell her about pain Lanh has. I tell her he have this pain many times. She write down what his pain mean."

Siu pulled out a note on which the nurse had written that Lanh has chronic ear infections and will need to take antibiotics everyday.

"Nurse give me medicine for Lanh," Siu continued. "She tell me I come back one week to check to see for more medicine."

Carrie nodded attentively, encouraging Siu to continue.

"I meet nurse again and she ask about children and family," Siu paused. "At first I not want to tell her what happen in my house. As wife I must keep these things inside, not bring shame to my family. I have much fear of what happen if I say something. So I tell nurse nothing. Two weeks later my son sick again so my husband send to clinic. When I see nurse again she ask me about children and husband," Siu continued.

"This day I very upset, my husband break dishes and memories from home, so I come and start cry. I tell her my husband cause me trouble, and she say come talk to you. I tell her I do not talk to someone. This dangerous. I tell her bring dishonor to my family to talk," Siu paused again, apparently thinking hard about what she was going to say next. "Nurse ask me if my kids safe. I not know what to say. That when I decide come talk to you. My husband think I at nurse when I here."

Carrie looked closely at Siu, surprised by the courage of this woman who appeared so frail just minutes earlier.

"What can you tell me about your relationship with your husband?" Carrie asked.

"We marry in Vietnam," Siu said, "I very young but he long friend of my family. Shortly after we married, he say his family live in United States and we move, too. We escape bad life in Vietnam after war. My family all stay in Vietnam."

For the next twenty minutes, Siu described an experience Carrie could have never imagined. Siu told of the journey, ten years before, from Vietnam. She seemed to recall it as if it were yesterday. In 1995 Siu and her husband had been some of the last refugees who traveled by way of a makeshift boat from Vietnam to the Philippines. The boat trip was dangerous and frightening. There was a constant threat of drowning or attack by notorious pirates. She told of being sick to her stomach from the storms, sickness, starvation, and dehydration that she and others had endured, all for eventual refuge in the United States. The boat was cramped and hot. When they arrived in the Philippines after three weeks, they were taken to a refugee camp in Palawan. Life in the camp was not wonderful, they were bored and frightened and always unsure about their future. But unlike Vietnamese refugees in some other countries, they were not beaten or tortured.

A year after Siu and her husband arrived at the camp, most refugees were being forced to return to Vietnam. Her husband was part of a large group that rioted at the airport when Philippine officials tried to force them to return. They feared persecution if they returned to Vietnam. Eventually, this group of refugees was allowed to stay in the Philippines indefinitely. Two years later, the president of the Philippines issued an order allowing Vietnamese asylum-seekers to seek permanent residency in the Philippines. Though many others living in the camp chose to do this, Siu's husband refused. He had a strong desire to reach the United States. Almost seven and a half years later, in 2005, Siu and her husband were finally processed as refugees by the United States and were resettled into the U.S. near Mr. Lee's family.

"I thought life would be easier now that I here," Siu said. But the adjustment to the change had been harder than she had anticipated. Her English was poor, and she had few opportunities to learn. She also missed her family and friends in Vietnam.

Siu also told Carrie about memories of her life in Vietnam. As a very young child, their home was full of family and friends, good food, and celebration of life. That time, according to her mother and her mother's friends, had been a period of good karma. As a Buddhist, Siu believed in karma, that whatever you do intentionally to others will happen to you in the future. She believed that her hardships were the result of something she had done in the past, and that she was destined to experience this.

"It must be hard for you to be here without your family and friends," Carrie said.

"It hard," Siu agreed. "I only few things to remember."

Siu told Carrie she had taken a few of her mother's things with her, some small jewelry, dishes, and dolls that she was able to keep safe. One small dish, bright yellow, reminded her of her mother's birthday celebration ten years before. These were some of the only mementos she had left of her mother and her past life in Vietnam.

"What else has made it difficult for you living here in the United States?" Carried questioned.

"My husband change," Siu continued. "He destroy my things I take from Vietnam." Siu paused, overwhelmed with emotion. "He turn crazy."

Siu described the years of isolation and pain caused by her husband. He did not allow her to leave the home alone except for a few rare instances like the appointments with the nurse to pick up medicine for Lanh. He left her alone with the children for long periods of time, not telling her where he was going or when he would return. Under no circumstances was she allowed to answer the telephone or the door. Siu continued with vivid details of the things she had so carefully packed to bring to the United States from Vietnam and how her husband destroyed them for no apparent reason.

When Siu described a time her husband urinated on a pile of her things, Carrie felt sick to her stomach. *The horrible things this woman had to endure,* she thought.

"My husband family here, his parents, brothers, they all here in United States for him," Siu continued. "When we arrive, he join his brothers in make own supermarket. He and brothers always at work, at least six days each week. I see my husband family for special days; they not care about me, no call or stop by house, only see my husband," Siu paused. "They treat me bad; tell me what do and not let me know anything. Family supposed to help. Family help each other. But me, I no have family like that. As wife, I have bad marriage," Siu said. "My family suffer, my life, I despair. I have shame for this."

Siu went on to explain how her fear of bringing shame upon her family had kept her from speaking out about her husband's abuse.

"In my country," Siu said, "we no talk about thing like this. We believe family higher. Me not hurt the name of family. Family stay together, that what most important. But now, I not know what to do. I no want to bring shame to family but not want live like this."

"I can see that you feel a lot of responsibility for your family," Carrie responded, "but is it right for your husband to be treating you this way? Does he not have some responsibility for honoring you? You should not have to feel scared in your own home. We can help you with these things. I can tell you about the programs we have and you can decide what you would like to do."

Siu nodded, apparently curious to hear what Carrie had to say.

Carrie described the counseling and family services that she and a counselor could provide. She also described the shelter program available for women and their children.

"This program," Carrie said, "might be a good place for you and your children to start. We provide a safe room for you and your children. You get support from case managers and other families living in the shelter."

Carrie noticed that Siu grew tense when she mentioned the shelter program for women and their children, and decided not to pursue it. Instead, she suggested they see each other once every other week with appointments coordinated with the health nurse to discuss how Siu was coping with her situation. Because it had taken Siu many hours to get the medicine the first time, her husband would not question her being gone for a long time. She and her sons would go first to the clinic to get the medicine for Lanh from the nurse and then come to see Carrie at My Sister's Place.

Siu agreed that this was a good plan and they scheduled an appointment for two weeks later.

Once Siu had left, Carrie decided she would look over some notes she had taken at a training a few weeks earlier on domestic violence and its relation to various cultural and religious beliefs. Carrie remembered the training had covered

Southeast Asian cultural and religious beliefs in relation to domestic violence and Carrie thought this would be good information to review before her next meeting with Siu.

The visit with Siu fresh in her mind, Carrie read over her notes with new appreciation. For example, she was reminded that, historically, domestic violence has been accepted and legitimized within Southeast Asian cultures. Southeast Asian communities and families are often patriarchal and conservative in their view of gender roles. This culture highly values honoring one's family. Because women have a large role in determining the reputation of their family, they are taught to honor their family at any cost, even if this includes silently suffering domestic violence. In this culture a woman should be unconditionally devoted to her husband, even if he is abusing her. Buddhism, the most popular religion of Southeast Asians, promotes the idea of karma. Karma is the philosophy that your current actions will determine your fate. How ever one intentionally treats others will determine how one is treated by others in the future. Hardships, like domestic violence, are often viewed as the result of one's past actions and therefore something deserved.

She also read that intimate partner violence is often prevalent within Southeast Asian communities living abroad. Among these communities, alcohol and drug use, gambling, mental illness, stress and frustration are factors which people use to explain intimate partner violence. Gender, class, age, culture, and immigration status can affect an abused Southeast Asian woman's attitude toward partner violence, her ability to protect herself and her family, and her ability to do anything else about her situation. Frequently, Southeast Asian women in America live in isolation and alienation from the outside world because of language and cultural barriers. These barriers can keep battered women from finding out what their options might be.

Finally, in reviewing the materials, Carrie remembered that if and when South Asian women seek support for their struggles with domestic violence, it is often informal support from friends and family. The women are often wary of and uncomfortable with formal, outside support from agencies. Among Southeast Asian communities, attitudes exist against calling the police or separating from one's abusive partner. Carrie learned that when helping women from this culture, a central concept should be that every woman has the right to assume control over her own life and the philosophy should be one of empowerment.

Tuesday Afternoon—Two Weeks Later

When Carrie walked down the hall to meet Siu for their third appointment, she noticed a small change in the woman's demeanor. Siu instructed her boys to head to the play area and "play nice," and turned and followed Carrie into her office.

"I tired," Siu began, "tired of him breaking my things, and yelling at me. I know you tell me of this shelter many times, but I afraid to go."

"The people who work there are wonderful and you will be safe from your husband," Carrie spoke.

"I cannot go," Siu countered, shaking her head, "I not refugee anymore, I lose everything if I go."

"I understand that those times were very hard for you," Carrie said.

"Yes," Siu replied, "I not have that pain again."

"What could I do to show you that it would not be like that again?" Carrie asked.

"No, no," Siu replied. "I not live like refugee again!"

Carrie suspected it would be impossible to convince Siu to stay in the shelter program because of her past experience and the horror this caused. She thought of the other housing programs in the city and what other options might be a good fit for Siu.

"There is a program we have not discussed," Carrie continued. "This program is called transitional housing. It's a two-year program provided by the federal government. It provides you and your boys a home, and education classes so you can learn things like paying your bills, getting a job, getting your driver's license, and enrolling your children in school. The workers help you for two years and then you are ready to live on your own."

"Do we have own place?" Siu asked.

"Yes, the program will give you your own home for two years," Carrie answered. "Sometimes it takes a long time to get into the program, but we could fill out the forms now and see what happens."

"Yes, I think good," Siu agreed. "I come meet you until move?" Siu questioned.

"Yes, I think we can still work together to make sure your family is safe until you move," Carrie agreed.

Tuesday Afternoon—Two Months Later

"Good news, Siu," Carrie said excitedly, as she and Siu sat down for their bi-weekly session, "You were accepted into the transitional housing program. We just need to wait until the next apartment opens up and you and your children will be able to move in and start the program."

"That great news," Siu beamed.

Carrie thought back to the day when she had first told Siu about the program. She was in so much pain, but was never able to commit to leaving until she knew she would have a safe place to live with her children. When problems got worse at home, Carrie sometimes reminded her of the shelter program that was available for her and her children. Nevertheless, Siu refused to go. She told Carrie the pictures of this place brought back the nightmares of her refugee experience coming to the United States. She could not, and would not put herself or her children into a place like this again. It had been horrible.

"This program, good choice for me and my children," Siu said, "we safe here not afraid."

Carrie nodded, thinking of how much this transitional housing program and potential opportunity had changed Siu's perspective toward life. She thought back to their bi-weekly sessions, and the stories Siu told of what went on in her home. Her husband refused to let her leave the house except for her appointments with the nurse. One evening, for no apparent reason, he broke her mother's jewelry into tiny pieces with a hammer. Carrie knew these things, mementos of the past, held so much value to Siu, and that Siu's heart was broken over and over again as he destroyed them.

"How long until go?" Siu asked.

"The program director, Ms. Carter, said it could be just one or two more weeks," Carrie replied.

Wednesday Afternoon

The next day, when Carrie checked her voicemail messages after lunch, she was surprised to hear a message from the transitional housing program director, Samantha Carter. Carrie called back immediately.

"We have a spot open immediately for Siu Lee," Samantha explained. "We just need a letter from your agency indicating her homeless status. That's a requirement for federal funding. But then she can move in."

"That's wonderful news, but," Carrie paused, "I need to talk to you about the homeless status letter. Siu is still living in her home, and has never stayed in a domestic violence shelter. She was a refugee from Vietnam and because of this has some serious issues with moving into a shelter."

"We have very strict guidelines for federal funding," Samantha replied, "and we must have a letter indicating the clients we accept into the program are currently in shelter programs and have homeless status. It doesn't matter how many nights she is in the shelter and I don't care how you get the letter. I just need to have a letter from your agency stating Siu has homeless status, and then she can move in."

As Carrie hung up the telephone, one question kept running through her mind: *Shall I write that letter? And what happens to Siu if I don't?*

4

GONE HUNTIN'

Sandy L. Bauer and Leslie S. Gregory

"I would just like to know," Roger Roberts said emphatically, "that she won't mess with my huntin'! I like to do a little huntin' every fall. It's something I've been doin' since I was a kid, way before I ever met Connie."

"I don't mind *a little* huntin'," Connie Roberts exclaimed, "but Roger starts huntin' in September and doesn't stop 'til December. He's gone almost every weekend and a whole week over Thanksgiving. I want to know that Roger will be there if I need him, even if it's during a huntin' trip. I need him to be available, if I need him . . . ," Connie paused, "no matter what. I need him to agree to come home from huntin' if there's an emergency or family happening that I feel requires his presence. I always take the backseat. I'm lonely and don't feel my needs are important to Roger."

Social worker Laura Adams sighed to herself. It was only her second marital counseling session with the Roberts but already she was wondering how this couple was going to see past their differences. Married for eight years, they evidently had some entrenched patterns. *What sacrifices might they be willing to make to start meeting each other's needs? Can they feel an intimate connection again? Is forgiveness and healing possible? How might faith help in this process?*

Family Counseling Services

Family Counseling Services (FCS) was founded in the 1980s as an outgrowth

Development of this decision case was supported in part by the University of South Carolina College of Social Work. It was prepared solely to provide material for class discussion and not to suggest either effective or ineffective handling of the situation depicted. While based on field research regarding an actual situation, names and certain facts may have been disguised to protect confidentiality. The authors and editors wish to thank the anonymous case reporter for cooperation in making this account available for the benefit of social work students and practitioners.

of a ministry of a local church in the Washington, DC, area. At its inception, it offered crisis counseling services to Christians in the local community. Over time, however, its services expanded as it began offering individual, family, and marital counseling services to clients of all ages (regardless of religious background or affiliation) in several geographic areas.

FCS employed approximately 100 social workers, psychologists, and other mental health professionals. Although no longer an exclusively Christian counseling organization, many of the therapists at FCS were Christians, encompassing a range of Christian traditions. Yet, other therapists were Jewish, Buddhist, or professed no religious affiliation.

Funded largely through insurance, with few cash clients, FCS experienced the effects of managed care as insurance companies paid for only a set number of sessions. Low insurance reimbursement rates and client co-payments were beneficial for insurance companies and for many clients, but meeting budgetary demands was often a challenge for FCS.

Most clients were referred to FCS through their insurance companies, Christian counseling referral programs, or by a physician, friend, or clergy. Referrals were taken by non-clinical intake staff at FCS. These staff gathered client demographic and insurance information as well as the reason for the referral. Following the brief telephone intake, clients were matched to therapists based on the clinician's area of specialty, availability, and the expressed needs of the client (e.g., preferred faith background, gender, marital, or parental status of therapist, evening or weekend appointments, payment method and ability). Therapists received a brief two-page intake with demographic information, insurance information, and the reason for referral. From this information, a therapist contacted the client to arrange an initial assessment.

Laura Adams

Laura Adams had BSW and MSW degrees and twelve years of practice experience in various clinical and supervisory positions in the child welfare field, including five years as a supervisor for a religiously affiliated child welfare agency. About the same time she began that position, she also began teaching social work practice courses part-time for a religiously affiliated baccalaureate social work program. She left the supervisory position in 2001 but, as a practice teacher, felt the need to resume social work practice again. She joined the staff at FCS in 2003 as a part-time clinical social worker out of desire to be more directly involved in clinical practice.

Laura started at FCS uncertain about what to expect. Most of her social work experience had been as a supervisor in child welfare. Clinical work was a new experience. Laura felt a mixture of anxiety, doubt (in her own abilities), enthusiasm, fear and excitement about her new role as a clinical social worker. Although she knew she could draw on her professional knowledge, she was also hoping that her thirteen-year marriage and her experience as a mother of four children would be of some help to her, especially in her work with women, couples, and families.

Laura had chosen FCS, in part, because of its religious roots. Laura grew up in a Christian home and was saved at a young age. She had a personal relationship with God and faith disciplines—prayer, devotions and fellowship with other believers—were important in her daily life. She regularly attended a large evangelical church. Although faith was very important to Laura personally, she was still considering how to address faith issues in her new work place.

In the early stages at FCS, she was concerned with learning about the agency, including understanding the paperwork and other policies and procedures. A particular concern for Laura was the assessment process that included giving each client a clinical diagnosis for insurance purposes. This was something Laura had never done. She wondered if she would recall content on the Diagnostic and Statistical Manual from the human behavior course she had taken 10 years earlier. Another concern related to her ability to use effective and meaningful interventive techniques. She felt confident in her ability to build rapport, care and trust, but wondered if clients would find their work together meaningful and helpful. In short, Laura wondered, *Am I truly prepared for the work I am about to begin?*

January 2003

As her first client, Laura was given a referral for Connie Roberts, a 46-year-old female, and her husband, Roger. The referral was for marital conflict. From the intake form Laura could see that the Roberts came to FCS because it accepted their insurance and was close to their home. She also noted they had not specifically requested a Christian counselor.

Laura contacted Ms. Roberts to arrange the first session. After determining whether this was a convenient time to talk, Laura introduced herself and scheduled an appointment with Connie and Roger. She gave Connie directions to the office, gave her some basic information about the initial session and noted that their insurance would cover 30 visits per calendar year. Laura explained that she would mail some paperwork for Connie and Roger to complete before the first session. She promised that she would meet the Roberts in the waiting room at the scheduled appointment time. Before concluding the call, Laura asked whether Connie had any questions or concerns. Connie mentioned that she and Roger were on the brink of separation because of unresolved marital issues.

Preparing To Meeting the Roberts

In preparation for the first session, Laura tuned in to her feelings and concerns about meeting the Roberts, in addition to imagining the potential feelings and concerns of the Roberts. Laura thought, *I am feeling so anxious. I don't know what to expect and I hope I will be able to meet the Roberts' needs.* Excitement also pervaded Laura, as she had a special interest in working with couples experiencing marital conflict. She looked forward to hearing the Roberts' story.

Laura thought more about her phone call with Connie. *She sounded pleasant on the phone, but also frustrated about her marriage, even hopeless.* Roger's willingness to come in for counseling was also on Laura's mind. She wondered, *Did Connie give him an ultimatum?* Laura wondered whether the Roberts had any previous experience with counseling.

Building rapport, trust and care was important to Laura as three elements of the helping relationship. She needed to formulate her role and purpose in this new setting, so she could explain this to the Roberts. She decided to use the three elements of the helping relationship as one way to express her role and purpose.

Laura planned a brief assessment for the initial session. The anxieties the Roberts brought to the first session also weighed on Laura's mind, as she expected that they were also concerned about what to expect from FCS, Laura, and from their work together. *I wonder if they will be as nervous as I am?*

Session One

Laura met Connie and Roger Roberts, a white couple, in their mid-40s, in the FCS waiting room. Connie was petite and attractive, but looked tired and worn down. Roger was of average size and build with red hair and fair complexion that looked a little flushed. *They look like a nice couple,* Laura thought, *but Connie barely shook my hand and Roger isn't making eye contact with me. I wonder what this means?*

As Laura led them into the office she said, "Please sit wherever you will be most comfortable."

The Roberts chose two adjacent chairs as opposed to sitting together on the small sofa. But Laura was so nervous that she hardly gave their choice of seating a thought.

"First I need a minute to look over the paperwork and review some things with you. Everything we talk about will be kept confidential unless you tell me to tell someone else, like your doctor, or if you are having thoughts of hurting yourself or someone else. I am also required to report concerns about child abuse. Do you have any questions about that?"

The Roberts both shook their heads no.

Laura continued, "Do you have any questions about all the paperwork you filled out? I know it is a lot to read and complete."

They both said, "No," and handed Laura their forms.

Laura quickly scanned the information on the personal data form (one of the forms that clients had to complete for the chart). Laura learned that there was a five-year age difference between Connie and Roger, with Connie being older. They had been married eight years. This was Roger's first marriage, while Connie had been married previously. They had no children. *I need to be sure,* Laura thought, *to explore Connie's first marriage and the reason they have no children.*

Both Connie and Roger were both employed as engineers at a pharmaceutical company. Laura recognized their home address. *A secluded and sought after community of higher priced homes,* Laura mused. *They likely have a comfortable lifestyle and lovely home.*

Connie had written, on the personal data form, that her faith was important to her. Laura wondered how this might become a part of her work with clients not specifically seeking Christian counseling. Laura thought, *It will be great to make this faith connection with Connie.* Connie listed the name of a local Protestant church, where she was currently a member. Roger wrote that he grew up Lutheran, but answered, "No" to the question of, "Is faith important to you?" Roger left the line blank where a client could list their current church or religious affiliation. Laura wondered, *Could the difference in how Connie and Roger describe the importance of faith in their life be a source of conflict for them?*

Also listed on the personal data form was the fact that the Roberts had been in counseling earlier in their marriage. Laura thought, *I need to be sure to explore this at some point.*

"Since I see that you have been in counseling before," Laura began, "you probably have a good idea of what we will be doing together. Tonight I want to hear from both of you about what brings you here so we can begin to establish some goals. By establishing goals we will better know how we are doing in our work together and know when we are reaching the end of our work. My primary job is to help build our relationship by helping you both feel heard and cared about. I am also here to help you talk and listen to one another so that you can learn to communicate better at home. I need to build trust between us because if you do not trust me, you won't be honest with me or with one another. Through all of this I hope that we will be able to work on the concerns that are bringing you here tonight. How does this sound?"

Both Connie and Roger said, "Fine."

"So," Laura continued, "who wants to start sharing what has been going on?"

Connie responded immediately, "We haven't been gettin' along. This is a problem every winter after huntin' season. I am always put on the back burner, while Roger goes off huntin'. He thinks he can go and do whatever he wants and he almost seems to forget that I'm at home all alone. "

Connie continued for nearly 10 minutes explaining her feelings about being left alone while Roger was hunting.

Roger remained quiet, rarely interjecting his side of the story even though Laura looked at him from time to time as Connie was talking. *Roger seems nervous and uncomfortable and he isn't really making much eye contact. Does Roger even want to be here, or is this how things usually go in the relationship, with Connie taking over?* She also quickly realized how hard it was to mediate between two people during a counseling session. *I need to figure out a way to engage him.*

When Connie paused, Laura turned to Roger and said, "It sounds like you are an avid hunter."

"Yeah," Roger responded, "I've been huntin' every fall, for as long as I can remember. At first I'd hunt with my Dad and brothers, and now it's with my brothers and friends."

As Roger continued, Laura thought, *Well, it is obvious that hunting is a passion of Roger's. It is great to see how his demeanor has changed. He is so excited and animated.* Connie, on the other hand, had grown quiet during this time and kept her arms crossed.

"So," Laura asked, "What are some of the things you like to do, Connie, while Roger is hunting?"

"Oh, I enjoy attendin' church, readin', cookin' and carin' for my, dog, Dusty.

He's like my baby, although he's already 12 years old. He's the one good thing that I got out of my first marriage."

"Well," Roger piped in, "I love Dusty too."

Connie agreed, "Yeah, he does."

Laura asked them what they liked to do together. They easily listed several things, including snowmobiling in the winter, gardening in the spring and summer, and winemaking in the fall.

"Having these common interests seems like a wonderful source of strength for you," Laura interjected.

Connie agreed, "Yeah, we do have our good points."

"I notice that you do not have any children," Laura commented, recognizing that this might be a difficult area to talk about.

"No," Connie slowly began, "I can't have children because of infertility problems. Five years ago we saw a counselor for several months and we dealt with all that then. I had in vitro about five years ago. But, it didn't work. I guess we are happy with our lives now even though a child would have been nice. I have always thought about bein' a Big Sister, but just have never done it."

Laura wondered, *Is the issue of not being able to have children really as resolved as Connie is presenting? She seems like she is trying to convince herself as well as me. Once we have developed more rapport and trust in our relationship I should address this.*

Laura continued the session by gathering a brief family history starting with Roger. She learned that Roger was the younger of two brothers, and came from a working class family with traditional gender roles.

"My mom stayed at home and took care of things around the house and all. My dad worked a lot." Roger stated.

"Were they close?" Laura asked.

"I guess," Roger responded, sounding ambivalent.

"How did your family display their feelings of love and care?" Laura asked.

"Well, we weren't too much into that kind of stuff. There weren't many hugs and all," Roger replied.

"What about verbally," Laura continued, "did your family tell each other 'I love you'?"

"No, but you just knew it," Roger defended.

Laura wondered, *Has this manner of relating been carried into the marriage? Roger doesn't even sit close to Connie or show any other signs of physical or verbal affection to Connie, although neither does she.* At that point, Laura recalled that they both seemed to avoid the sofa when offered their choice of seats.

Laura continued gathering a family history with Connie.

Connie shared that she was the youngest of three children, with two older brothers.

"My parents divorced when I was an infant. My mom worked all the time and my grandmother really is the one who raised me," Connie stated.

"What was your relationship like with your dad?" Laura asked.

"Well, there really was no relationship. I never saw him much. My mom was working all of the time. Thank God for my grandmother. She's the one who taught me to cook and sew. She was just a loving, Godly woman," Connie replied.

Laura wondered, *Might this relationship be the source from which Connie's faith was sparked and nurtured?*

"What about your mom?" Laura interjected.

Connie laughed, "Well, she is another story all together. We could take up years of sessions talkin' about her. She is a bitter, angry woman. She really is no support to me. I know she loves me, but she is so angry all the time and she really doesn't seem to know how to show love."

Laura nodded and paused, wondering about how Connie's family impacted her actions in her marriage. She thanked Connie and Roger for sharing their stories and asked them where they wanted to go from here.

Connie told Laura, "I'm at the end of my rope. We never talk to each other. I am not even sure I want the relationship. I know I don't want it like it is now. We fight a lot and we never seem to be able to work it out."

"Maybe we should end it," Roger sounded hopeless.

Laura nodded, "I hear that you are both struggling with the way things are right now and how they have been. Is a divorce or a separation something that either of you want?"

They both shook their heads and replied, "No."

Laura continued, "I know things may feel hopeless right now, but I believe there is a lot of hope for your future. It is going to be a journey of ups and downs, but you already have strengths that we can build on as we work together on the areas that are causing you to struggle and making you feel like you want to end things."

Laura knew it was time to bring the session to an end, "All that you have shared with me tonight has been helpful for me to start to get to know you and what you are struggling with. I am wondering if you would like to come back next week to continue our work together."

They both nodded and said, "Yes." To Laura's surprise, Roger added quietly, "That would be a good idea."

Laura continued, "Since we are running out of time for tonight, we will talk more next week about goals. By next week I would like you each to individually write down some goals that you have for our work together. It might help for you to think of it this way, 'How will you know when we are done? What will be different in your marriage?'"

Again, they both nodded and said, "Okay."

Laura scheduled an appointment for next week. She felt uncomfortable about asking for the co-pay, but knew she needed to collect it.

"So, how would you like to pay your co-pay?"

Connie said, "Oh, we have cash, it's $10, right?"

Laura responded, "Yes, that's right," and took the money from Connie.

They exchanged goodbyes and the Roberts left.

Laura was relieved the session was over and thought to herself, *That wasn't so bad.* She now had to begin the task of filling out the authorization form required by the insurance company, which included a history, five-axis diagnosis, mental status exam, and social system stressors evaluation. She felt a twinge of doubt in her ability to do this, realizing how independent and accountable you have to be when working in this field.

As she worked through the paperwork she reflected on how hopeless the Roberts both seemed to feel. *What might be the hurts,* she wondered, *that keep them from meeting one another's needs? How can I help them reconnect and want to invest energy into their marriage again?*

Session Two

In the next session, after hearing about their goals, Laura explored the source of their conflicts, as they both shared the goal of wanting to more effectively deal with their conflicts and to learn to get along better.

Laura asked, "What are your individual needs and what do you need from each other?"

"I would just like to know," Roger responded, "that she won't mess with my huntin'. I like to do a little huntin' every fall. It's something I've been doin' since I was a kid, way before I ever met Connie."

"I don't mind *a little* huntin'," Connie exclaimed and then continued angrily and in a loud voice, "but Roger starts huntin' in September and doesn't stop 'til December. He's gone almost every weekend and a whole week over Thanksgivin'."

Laura thought, *Can the clients in the waiting room hear Connie? She is talking so loud right now. I wonder if Connie gets angry with Roger like this often?* Laura was about to interject, as she felt that she needed to somehow protect Roger, but then Connie's tone softened and her voice lowered.

"I want to know that Roger will be there if I need him even if it's durin' a huntin' trip; I need him to be available, if I need him…no matter what. I need him to agree to come home from huntin' if there's an emergency or family happenin' that I feel requires his presence. I always take the backseat. I'm lonely and don't feel my needs are important to Roger," Connie said.

"Here she goes with 'the switch'," Roger interjected loudly. "She starts off agreein' to my huntin' and then gets all mad."

Laura looked at Connie, whose jaw dropped. She looked like she had been slapped by Roger's comment. Laura felt put on the defensive for Connie. *That sounds hurtful and even sexist,* Laura thought.

"I don't want Connie to decide whether I need to come home from huntin'," Roger continued. "I will come home if I think I need to. I don't need Connie tellin' me what to do."

Laura's thoughts stayed with Connie. *I need to choose my response wisely,* Laura thought, *because Roger's statement is really making me want to side with Connie.* Laura didn't want to alienate Roger, but as a wife she could understand how these words must hurt Connie.

"How do you express these needs to one another?" Laura inquired.

"Well," Connie began slowly, "we either fight about it or just quit talkin' all together."

"What happens when these needs aren't met?" Laura asked.

This was met with a lot of silence, to which Laura conjectured, "You just want to give up." Connie and Roger nodded in agreement.

Laura wondered, *Do they see the difficulty they are having with communication, problem solving and compromise?* Laura heard their frustration and lack of desire to meet one another's needs. *How can I help them establish healthier communication patterns? I know gaining insight into these problems and beginning to heal is going to be a long process, but I am not even sure what to say next.* Relief fell over Laura as she heard Connie's voice break the silence.

"One of the in vitro treatments was during huntin' season, and Roger acted like he wasn't goin' to come home for it. I felt like I really needed him and was just always bein' put on the back burner," Connie complained.

Roger interjected, "Why did the in vitro have to be planned durin' huntin' season?"

Connie was quick to respond, "Why is huntin' more important than tryin' to have a baby?"

Laura's thoughts began to consume her as she listened to Connie and Roger, *As a wife and mother, it is hard for me to imagine hunting being more important than trying to have a baby. Did Roger ever really want a baby? Or did he just not know how to express his care and concern for Connie during this difficult time? Was Roger hurting too when the in vitro didn't work? Although Connie had the in vitro on schedule, does she still place some blame for it not being successful on Roger and his hunting.*

"I did get pregnant once," Connie went on, "it actually wasn't durin' the in vitro, but a few months after treatment."

Sensing her hesitation Laura asked, "Do you want to talk about what happened?"

Connie responded slowly, "I had a miscarriage. I wasn't that far along."

"I can only imagine how painful that must have been," Laura said empathically.

"Yeah, it was hard," agreed Connie.

"How was it for you, Roger?" Laura asked.

Roger quickly responded, "Oh, I dealt with it okay."

Laura saw the hurts and struggle between the Roberts. *I am not sure,* she thought, *what Roger's statement of 'I dealt with it okay' really means. Part of me sees Roger as cold and uncaring and another part sees him as struggling to support and care for Connie, while coping with his own feelings of sadness and loss.* Laura's thoughts continued, *Given Roger's upbringing maybe talking about feelings and showing how he feels, particularly sadness, might not have been encouraged. Maybe this really is hard for him. How can I help bring healing to both of them about this difficult and painful loss that they both seem to still be carrying around?* Laura felt overwhelmed, inadequate and uncertain of the next step.

Noticing the time, Laura ended the session and scheduled their next appointment.

"See you next week," Roger said as he got up. Connie stood, handed Laura $10 and thanked her as she followed Roger out the door.

Sessions Three to Five

Over the next several sessions, Connie and Roger shared more of their story with Laura, including how they met and what first attracted them to one another. They also discussed more of the issues surrounding past hurts and the dynamics of their relationship over time. Laura continued to reflect during these sessions how much it seemed they were holding onto the past and not able to forgive each other.

Session Six

Roger and Connie arrived early to their sixth session reporting that they had had an argument.

"Do you want to talk about the specifics of the argument or do you feel you were able to resolve it?" Laura asked.

Laura felt anxious as Connie and Roger sat silent at first. Finally, Connie responded by asking Roger, "Do you want to start or should I?"

"Go ahead," Roger deferred.

"Roger wanted to have sex last night," Connie began, "and I was so tired. Roger became angry and sulked when I told him I was tired."

"Well," Roger interjected, "you're always tired."

"Yeah," Connie acknowledged, "I am tired a lot."

Boy, can I relate to that, Laura thought, *particularly as a mother of four young children. I'm exhausted too!*

After a long silence, Laura asked, "Is that all that the argument was about? Because, if you are tired at night, what about having sex early in the evening. Would that be possible for you guys?"

"Yeah that is somethin' we could do," they both agreed in unison.

Laura prodded, "What about my question about if there is something more to the argument? Because it seems to mirror previous discussions we have had around your struggle to meet each other's needs." Laura paused and then asked, "Roger, what are you thinking right now?"

"I guess I need to learn when to leave Connie alone." Roger replied.

"Is this what you want, Connie?" Laura asked.

"No, I am sayin' that I was tired and that sex isn't the only way to feel close." Connie said.

"Connie, what do you think Roger needs?" Laura asked.

"Sex, like any man," Connie responded quickly.

Laura saw Roger shift in his seat and make what Laura thought to be an understandably annoyed sigh.

Connie continued, "Don't get me wrong, I enjoy sex when we have it, but not when I am tired and no matter what Roger says, I am not always tired."

Laura responded, "Sex is one of the ways that a couple can be intimate and feel close. It is also something that can pull couples apart. Withholding it is often a way to get back at one another or to keep one another at a distance. I realize this might be difficult to talk about, but I am wondering what you think about this?"

"Honestly," Connie responded, "I do sometimes reject Roger's advances when I don't want to have sex, because I am hurt or mad at him and not just when I am tired."

"Yet, do you see how this could be one way to feel close?" Laura asked. "When you are hurting and upset you don't feel connected to Roger and so you withhold sex. You don't end up getting the closeness with Roger that you need and the result is that you feel even more disconnected."

"Yeah, but I just don't want him to think that everythin' is okay when it's not," Connie admitted.

How can I help her see that open communication and forgiveness will build more of a connection? Connie just seems to want to hold grudges.

"Roger, do you understand that Connie doesn't want to have sex when things don't feel right between you? When Connie doesn't feel emotionally connected with you, like when she is upset with you, she is less interested in sex." Laura explained.

"Yeah, I know," Roger conceded.

As the discussion continued, Roger and Connie seemed to gain some insight about their lack of intimacy, but they were still missing vital pieces. *Where does forgiveness come into play?* Laura wondered.

Since it was almost time for the session to end, Laura summarized what they had discussed and reviewed their homework for the week that related back to the fight they had.

After the session Laura began to wonder, *How can I help Connie and Roger feel an intimacy again? Is it possible to shift their selfish focus to a focus on each other? Do they want to experience healing in their marriage? They have such a difficult time with communication and telling one another what they need with all of these approach-avoidance tactics. How can I help them feel connected again?*

Laura shifted her thinking and began to wonder, *Would Connie's faith be a po-*

tential source of support and a way to help them reconnect? Since Roger does not place the same significance on his religious beliefs as Connie, would Roger see his spirituality as a source of support and help or even as a way of connecting with Connie during this marital crisis? Should I even explore the spiritual realm, as this will likely be positive and helpful for Connie, but potentially uncomfortable and alienating for Roger?

Session Seven

"We have talked in the past," Laura began, "about the importance of church in your lives. I'm wondering how this might help you feel united?"

Both nodded but neither said a word.

"I know, Roger, you've told me you do not attend church regularly and faith is not important to you," Laura said.

"That's right," Roger replied. "I don't attend church right now, except on holidays."

"I attend church regularly," Connie interjected, "except in the winter when we are away a lot. Church is really important to me. I pray all the time and it is helpful to me."

"See," Roger continued, sounding exasperated, "this is the thing I just don't understand . . . Oh, forget it, I'm not gonna go there."

I have no idea if this is going to be positive or negative, and it might hurt Connie, but Roger needs to continue sharing his thoughts if we are ever going to get anywhere.

"Roger, go ahead and share," Laura encouraged. "It sounds like something important."

After a brief pause, Roger continued, "I am not tryin' to put her down or anything, but I just don't understand how she can go to church every Sunday and then act that way."

"What is 'that way'?" Laura prodded.

"Well, you know, it's the 'switch' I have talked about before," Roger remarked, "and when it turns on she gets mad and the things that come out of her mouth, you know, cursin' and all."

"He's right, I do get mad and curse," Connie admitted. "I know it's wrong and I feel bad about it. I pray and ask God to help . . ."

"It doesn't make sense to me," Roger interrupted, "I can't understand it."

"I'm sure it doesn't make sense to God and that He doesn't like it either," Connie volunteered.

"Fortunately," Laura inserted, "God sees past our imperfections."

But even as she spoke, Laura wondered whether Roger felt this comment was directed at him. *Should I spend some time now talking about forgiveness, as one way toward healing and a feeling a unity?*

After a brief pause, Laura turned towards Roger and said, "I'm guessing that if you see Connie cursing and not living in a godly way that it is hard to see the benefits of her going to church."

"Yeah," Roger acknowledged, and silence pervaded the room again.

Laura remarked, "Can you think of ways that your faith might be a source of cohesion?"

Connie thought for a while and then said, "Well, I would love to get Roger to read Christian books with me. I read them all the time and they are really helpful, but I know that won't happen. It would be great if he would come to church with me."

"I just don't see the point in goin'," Roger shrugged. "I should move my membership to Connie's church, but I just haven't yet."

"I am wondering if you don't see the point," Laura responded, "because you don't see certain things in Connie's life and she goes to church regularly."

After Laura said this she wondered, *Should I have just said that? Am I implying that going to church means we will behave in certain ways? Am I just giving Roger more fuel for his argument?*

"Yeah," Roger responded quickly, "I just can't see how she goes there and is the way she is with the cursing and all."

"I don't disagree that it is wrong and I pray about it," Connie responded.

"Since you mention praying, what about that, is that something that you ever do together?" Laura questioned.

"We haven't," Connie said hesitantly.

Laura thought, *Roger is shifting in his seat. He isn't making eye contact with me now. I am touching on those uncomfortable issues again.*

"These can be uncomfortable issues to discuss," Laura interjected beginning to feel uncomfortable herself.

Roger nodded, confirming for Laura that he was not comfortable and that she had touched on a sensitive area. Laura's thoughts began to race and she felt her heart beat right along with those thoughts, *Should I explore this nod? He seems uncomfortable. I am feeling uncomfortable, too. Maybe I should just go back to restating why we are discussing the issue of faith and not process his nonverbal cues. But, will this seem evasive, uncaring or defensive? What would be helpful at this point?*

But Laura proceeded, "Again, I bring this up because I think it is important to consider all aspects of our lives as we work together and to explore the ways these aspects bring cohesion and strain."

There was silence from Connie and Roger.

Laura's nagging, racing thoughts returned, *The session is almost over and I am running out of time to pull all of these loose ends together . . . Why aren't they responding? Is it because I have touched on a taboo? Am I even making sense? How can I stay connected with both Connie AND Roger and bring the session to an end?*

Laura continued, "I also believe that the argument you had last week regarding sex provides another opportunity to incorporate concepts from your faith. That is the idea of forgiveness and it's something I want to talk more about in the next session."

They both replied, "Okay."

As Connie and Roger left her office, Laura was not sure how to help them through their current impasse. Laura thought, *They seem to keep adding bricks to a wall that they are building between them. With each hurtful word and unmet need another brick gets added.*

Laura pondered, *How can I use the idea of forgiveness to help them? They are both hurting. Is reconciliation and healing possible? Are they ready for this? Are they willing to offer forgiveness to one another? How do I even go about suggesting this? There are so many hurts and pains from early in their marriage to today. Is forgiveness really a possibility?*

5

Not My Church!

CLifford J. M. Rosenbohm

"You're not acting as my church acts!" church social worker Sandy Potts exclaimed. "In fact, you're not acting as His church would act!"

Peter Wilson, Senior Executive Director of Creekside Christian Church, and Rita Kimball, an assistant from human resources had just informed Sandy that she was being terminated. They had given the same news to others on the church staff as they met at fifteen minute intervals; another pair of administrators was doing the same in an adjoining room.

Creekside Christian Church

In October 2003, Creekside Christian Church was the 15th largest church in the United States. Attendance ranged from 8,000 to 12,000 weekly. A staff of approximately 115 people was housed in two locations. The main campus of the church sat just outside the city of Knoxville, Tennessee, with a second location of offices on Corporate Drive, a suburban office park where many businesses were also located. The church had grown fairly quickly over the previous 8 years.

However, Creekside had a longer history in this area. The church began in 1956 as a church plant, or a "daughter church" as it was referred to then. The first senior pastor, Charles R. Bates, served the church for 40 years, retiring on January 1, 1996. During Rev. Bates' tenure, the church moved to a 20-acre site outside the

Development of this decision case was supported in part by the University of South Carolina College of Social Work. It was prepared solely to provide material for class discussion and not to suggest either effective or ineffective handling of the situation depicted. While based on field research regarding an actual situation, names and certain facts may have been disguised to protect confidentiality. The author and editors wish to thank the anonymous case reporter for cooperation in making this account available for the benefit of social work students and practitioners.

city of Knoxville. Since 1992, the church had made several additional property purchases and now had a total of 115 acres. The second senior pastor, David Evans, began his tenure on January 2, 1996 and served the church until resigning effective September 1, 2003 to take another position at an even larger church. During this time church attendance grew from around 3,000 to 8,000 people participating in weekend services. The third senior pastor, Gary Lawson, began working at Creekside in July 2000 as the Adult Discipleship associate minister. He moved into the senior pastor's position starting September 3, 2003, after a unanimous vote from the Elder Board and an affirmative vote by the congregation.

As the church grew it started new churches in the Knoxville area. Three new church plants had a combined average attendance of 2,300. The purpose of Creekside says, "We exist to love God and to love people" and the church appeared to take this purpose seriously. The size of the church was some indication of its commitment to reaching out to people. Ministry programs covered the entire lifespan from nursery to seniors. Categories for ministry included traditional programs for children, youth, college students, and adults, as well as programs for families with special needs, Hispanic ministry, sports outreach, and music. The Care Ministry Department provided for a variety of needs both within the church and to the larger community. For example, the Department provided financial assistance and material resources such as clothing, food, furniture, appliances, and cars. The church social worker disbursed between $100,000-120,000 annually to people in need. The church gave another $1,000,000 to missions each year.

The cost of growth and providing such a broad array of ministries to the congregation and the community came with a price tag. The church has recently incurred a $16,000,000 debt for a new building project. Decisions had to be made on how to address this debt and the ongoing issues of growth the church was continuing to experience. The new senior pastor inherited these challenges and had a mandate from the Elder Board to come up with "X-amount of dollars" to alleviate the financial debt the church had incurred.

Things were changing at the church. Leaders informed staff and church members they were making progress on reducing the church's indebtedness. The budget would be changed to reflect the tight times. The percentage of the budget allowed for missions and benevolence would be decreased. There were plans to renovate parts of the church that had been rented out to a school. Staff from the Corporate Drive office had met with facilities staff to pick out offices on the main campus. Because the budget constraints also had implications for staff levels, the elders and new senior pastor began reviewing the structure of the current staff to determine whether there should be any restructuring. Nevertheless, as they began to make decisions concerning staff, church leaders told people, "This is not a financial decision; this is just restructuring and simplifying because of duplication of jobs."

Sandy Potts, BSW

Sandy Potts was the Associate Director of Care Ministry, essentially the church's social worker, and had been working at Creekside for more than three years. Now in her 50s, she had previously worked in a variety of professional capacities. After Sandy received a bachelor's of social work (BSW) from Asbury College in 1971, she and her husband, Bill, served about 20 years with OMS International, known formerly as the Oriental Missionary Society. They spent most of their time in Quito, Ecuador. As a result of their long experience overseas, Sandy and Bill were bilingual, speaking both Spanish and English fluently. After returning from the mission field, they became heavily involved in the Spanish ministry at Creekside. In addition, Sandy volunteered at a crisis pregnancy center for three years and directed a crisis pregnancy center for one year, taught a sexual abstinence curriculum in public schools for four years, and worked at a community action council for eight months just before beginning at the church.

As Associate Director of Care Ministries at Creekside, Sandy had an important and multifaceted role in the congregation. She administered the benevolence program, which provided financial assistance for rent, utilities, food and other dry goods. She worked directly with clients to develop six-month care plans around a variety of presenting issues. These clients included both church members and others from the community. Sandy provided periodic training for church staff members who did not know how to work with people who came to the church for assistance. Sandy had trained twenty-five volunteers in various Care Ministry programs as volunteer caseworkers. Subsequently, she coordinated, scheduled, and supervised these volunteers. Sandy also supervised social work and counseling students from local universities in field practica at Creekside. Finally, Sandy managed several annual church programs like the food drive and Thanksgiving baskets for needy families in the community.

Sandy's lifelong relationship to the church and her passion for service, as both a minister and a social worker, framed her response to the recent actions and decisions happening at Creekside. Sandy was raised in a non-Christian home. Through the influence of an older sister, Sandy and her siblings began attending church. Home life was not always stable and for Sandy it was the model of Christ that she saw in her siblings that led her to depend on God. As a teenager she began to date the pastor's brother. This relationship affected Sandy's relationship to the church in another way. While dating, Sandy got pregnant. Her boyfriend wanted her to get an abortion and the family doctor advised her to get an abortion. With no one to turn to, Sandy came to understand the reality of Jesus in her life. Through the services of an unwed mother's home run by the Salvation Army, Sandy was able to surrender her son for adoption. The common practice at this time was for the child to be born and placed almost immediately with its adoptive family. When Sandy insisted on seeing her child, however, the social workers reluctantly allowed her to spend 30 minutes with him. Initially, they told Sandy that she could not do this because she would never go through with the adoption plan if she spent time with the child. But she was determined to do this and felt like it was very cathartic for her. Sandy wanted to let her son know what she was doing. She told him, "I want to make something out of my life so that if we ever meet you will see God's hand at work." This experience as an unwed pregnant teenager motivated Sandy to become a social worker. It allowed her to relate to other young girls as she served with her husband leading Bible studies at an unwed mother's home. She was able to share the grace of God with girls who were in the same position she had been in many years earlier. These opportunities gave Sandy a chance to share the hope of Christ and the healing that she knew the Church was supposed to give to those in need.

Decision time

The day began as many others had except that when Sandy walked through the doors of the Corporate Drive office building she noticed how quiet it was on her floor. There were about 35 staff members housed in this building on three different floors. No one else was on her floor except the receptionist. "They're having a meeting, they're upstairs and they're all crying, and it has something to do with a phone message. You should go to that meeting," the receptionist directed. Sandy decided to listen to the phone message before she did anything else. There had already been talk about people losing their jobs. The new senior pastor, 29-year-old Gary Lawson, and the church's senior executive director, Peter Wilson, had reassured staff members at the general staff meeting the month before: "You are the very best staff and no one will be let go until we take other steps."

Immediately after arriving at her office, Sandy checked for messages. "Sandy, we need you to come to the 'Decision Room' for a meeting at 4:45," the administrative assistant from Human Resources said on a telephone message. Trying to keep a positive outlook on what was happening, Sandy decided to go upstairs to where other staff members who had gotten a similar message were meeting. They were crying and praying. Sandy's boss, Bob Smart, was there.

Someone asked, "Did you get a message?"

"Yes," Sandy responded, "does that mean that I'm going to lose my job?"

"I don't think everyone will lose their jobs," someone else said, "but I'm sure that most of us will."

For her part, Sandy tried to be reassuring, reminding others in the room that God would take care of them all. After talking, crying and praying together the group finally disbursed and people tried to go on with the tasks of the day.

It was very difficult to concentrate on work that day. As the day progressed, people returning from the individual appointments in the Decision Room made comments like, "I'm out of here."

When Sandy asked several colleagues when they would be leaving, each of them said, "Today." Sandy could not believe what she was hearing. People were quietly packing up their offices. It all seemed incongruent to her. This was so totally foreign to the way she operated and thought about how people should be treated. Sandy did not pack any of her belongings. She thought, *that's so silly.*

Nevertheless, as 4:45 pm approached, Sandy felt rising anxiety. She left for the meeting with some trepidation.

Termination

"So, I guess I'm your next victim," Sandy said nervously as she sat down to meet with Peter Wilson and Rita Kimball.

"We're sorry that we're going to have to terminate your job," Peter Wilson said without further explanation.

"I don't understand," Sandy said, shocked at what she was hearing.

"Well, we're just having to cut back on some jobs, and where there is duplication . . ."

"There's no duplication of my job," Sandy interrupted emphatically, "no one else is doing it."

"Well," Peter responded firmly, "this is what we're going to have to do."

Questions came rushing into Sandy's mind and then came pouring out of her mouth just as quickly. "What about my clients who are coming in for pre-scheduled appointments on Monday? We have appointments already set for next week."

"Rita will take care of it," Peter replied, motioning toward her.

"What about the Thanksgiving program and the food drive next weekend?" Sandy asked.

"Rita will take care of them," Peter repeated.

We have to make decisions about what help clients need on Monday. Clients would be coming in for help. "What about the cases? What about the volunteers?" Sandy asked. "I work with fragile people who have suffered a lot of losses. You cannot just drop them like this."

"We'll take care of it," Peter promised. Then he changed the subject. "We really want you and your husband to keep coming to the church. You're invaluable to us."

"You're not acting as my church acts," Sandy exclaimed. "In fact, you're not acting as His church would act! This isn't the way the church is supposed to work. What about some other options you said you were going to do first?" Sandy questioned.

"We've looked at everything and this is what we're going to do," Peter answered. After a bit more conversation, he gave Sandy a packet of severance information.

"Thanks," Sandy said, as she stood to leave the room.

It was 4:55 pm when she checked her watch, shocked by what had just happened. Without prior notice, it was now Sandy's turn to clear out her office.

The Aftermath

As Sandy returned to her office, questions flooded her mind. *Have I done something wrong? My evaluations were always good. Don't they understand how important this work is to the mission of the church? Haven't I communicated effectively what the Care Ministry Department does?*

Then Sandy's thoughts turned toward how the church had behaved toward her in this situation. It brought back memories of some of her earlier encounters with the church as a teenager. *This is such an uncaring, disrespectful way to treat people!*

As Sandy rehearsed what had happened and imagined what the consequences might be, she faced several dilemmas and questions. Although Sandy's termination was effective immediately, she struggled with what to do with clients scheduled for appointments on Monday and throughout the coming weeks. *As a professional social worker,* Sandy thought, *I have a primary responsibility to my clients. Even if the church leaders do not understand the consequences of their actions on vulnerable people, I have to do something. Maybe I should go directly to the senior pastor or the elders to discuss these concerns. They just don't know what and how much we do in the Care Ministry Department.*

Other, more personal thoughts quickly raced through her mind, too. *What do I say to people I worship with, who want to know what's going on? How much do I tell them? How much do I not tell them? Who will supervise the practicum students?* This is *such a poor witness to the professional community and the universities where my practicum students come from. Can we continue going to church here?* But as she cleared out her office, the one thing that continued to push its way back into her thoughts was the clients. *What should I do about all those people already scheduled for next week? What will happen to them?*

While continuing to pack, Sandy rehearsed what she had said in the termination interview: *You're not acting as my church acts; in fact, you're not acting as His church would act. This isn't the way the church is supposed to be.* As Sandy mulled over the situation, another thought emerged: *The Church is supposed to be a place of healing and hope; not a place where hurt is given out.* Out loud, she asked herself, "What are you going to do about it?"

6

In Good Faith

F. Matthew Schobert, Jr.

"Louis is unaccounted for," executive director Pete Langen announced in his characteristically laconic New England manner. It was typical of his ability to say a mouthful with just a few words. It was the September, 2002, meeting of Food for All's Board of Directors and Pete's comment, brief though it was, immediately captured everyone's attention.

"What do you mean, 'unaccounted for'?" Brenda Rivas asked. A note of caution echoed in her voice.

"Unaccounted for," shrugged Pete, apparently unsure of what else to say. "He hasn't returned to Jacmel but he's not at CIRAD. I spoke with Blaise a couple days ago and asked about Louis. Blaise said Louis never returned home. So I called CIRAD to see if he was still there doing additional training, but they said he was not there and had never even arrived."

A disturbing quiet settled over the group. Pete finally uttered what everyone feared, "It doesn't look like Louis is going back to Haiti."

After an uncomfortable pause, Allison Crane broke the silence, "Well, aren't we going to report this to INS?" Her tone of voice was clear; she was charting a course of action, rather than voicing a question for discussion. Brandon Dicorte's level of unease sky rocketed.

Development of this decision case was supported in part by funding from the University of South Carolina College of Social Work. It was prepared solely to provide material for class discussion and not to suggest either effective or ineffective handling of the situation depicted. While based on field research regarding an actual situation, names and certain facts may have been disguised to protect confidentiality. The author and editors wish to thank the anonymous case reporter for co-operation in making this account available for the benefit of social work students and instructors.

Revised from Schobert, M. (2003). In good faith. *Social Work & Christianity, 30*(2), 178-188. Copyright © 2003 NACSW.

Food for All

Food for All (FFA) was a faith-based, non-profit organization of Christian volunteers and professionals committed to the alleviation of global hunger. It was started in 1974 by an ecumenical partnership of agricultural missionaries from the Mennonite Central Committee (MCC) and the United Methodist Committee on Relief (UMCOR). FFA, located in central Louisiana, just north of Alexandria, worked toward its mission by providing training, education, and on-site assistance in sustainable agricultural development, appropriate technologies for resource-poor communities in developing countries, and conservation. The bulk of FFA's funding came from individual donors, churches, and local foundations; but FFA also operated a number of income-generating projects, such as a community-supported organic garden and a fair-trade store that offered coffees, teas, and a wide variety of handmade goods from artisans in developing countries. FFA conducted community education, awareness, and outreach programs for the local and regional community. The centerpiece of their work, however, was training interns who would practice and teach sustainable agriculture in rural international settings.

FFA recruited domestic and international candidates for 15- and 12-month internships, respectively. FFA was not a sending agency; it did not sponsor, commission, or financially support international development workers. Domestic interns, therefore, typically came to FFA from Christian or humanitarian mission or relief and development agencies, often through connections with MCC or UMCOR, for fifteen months of training and education. Domestic interns spent nine months at Food for All, followed by three months at an on-site FFA agricultural development partnership program at one of four locations in Central America. Interns completed their training with a three-month capstone experience back at FFA where they integrated their work in Central America with their training at FFA. They also reflected upon and shared their on-site agricultural experiences with others at FFA and with local community organizations.

International interns came from countries around the world, particularly tropical countries in Central America, Sub-Saharan Africa, and South-Central Asia for a twelve-month internship program. These interns went through the same application process as domestic interns. They completed a lengthy application packet that required detailed personal information, educational background, professional skills, work experience, and a list of references. Applicants also had to write brief responses to six essay questions and an additional essay describing why they wanted to intern at FFA, what they hoped to learn, and how they planned on using what they learned after completing the internship. In addition to all of this, international interns were required to secure an H-3 visa to enter the United States. H-3 visas permitted international interns to enter the U.S. temporarily to receive education and training. These visas lasted the duration of a training program, but could not exceed two years. FFA assisted international applicants with the application process and the agency paid all fees and expenses for an H-3 twelve-month business-training visa. At the end of the twelve-month period, international interns returned to their home countries and introduced the training and education they learned from FFA to their local communities.

International interns made several unique contributions to FFA's mission. First of all, these interns "internationalized" FFA. They provided unique opportunities for FFA staff, volunteers, supporters, and especially domestic interns to interact with and learn from people of other cultures. This process began preparing domestic interns for cross-cultural experiences and challenges they would face when they traveled to their host country. International interns also represented, to FFA supporters and to local and regional communities, the driving purpose of the organization—to work toward the alleviation of hunger in developing countries. These interns also made unparalleled contributions to FFA's work because they generally represented key leaders and decision-makers in their communities of origin. International interns were embedded in the history, culture, and values of their communities and countries. They possessed keen awareness of their communities' strengths and weaknesses, of local assets and needs, and they could often identify what agricultural practices and technological interventions would or would not work in those contexts. Plus, international interns shared their knowledge of agricultural methodology, practice, and skills with FFA staff and domestic interns, enriching and expanding the agency's knowledge base and skill set.

Perhaps the single most important aspect of hosting international interns was that, upon returning to their homes, they were naturally viewed as "one-of-the-community." They were indigenous, insiders rather than outsiders. This bypassed a myriad of cross-cultural and relationship-building obstacles common in international relief and development work. Additionally, because international interns were returning home, their level of investment and commitment usually far exceeded that of domestic interns whose work, while crucial, often lasted for only a matter of months or years, as opposed to decades and generations. In their efforts to alleviate global hunger and reduce poverty, FFA staff and supporters understood that international interns represented the most effective and efficient use of the agency's limited resources.

Brandon Dicorte, LMSW

Although Brandon Dicorte was the newest FFA staff member, he had a long history with the organization. Brandon had attended Louisiana College, a small, liberal arts, Christian university located outside of Alexandria. Brandon majored in social work and public administration. During his years as an undergraduate, he volunteered at FFA through community service programs at Louisiana College and with members of Hope Chapel, a small, non-denominational congregation he attended. After college Brandon enrolled in a graduate social work program at Tulane University in New Orleans. He earned his masters degree in social work with a concentration in healthcare and started working in pediatric oncology at Tulane University Hospital and Clinic. Three years later he returned to Alexandria when Laura, his wife, began her medical residency program at Community Family Practice, a holistic healthcare clinic that served low-income and uninsured people and families. Shortly after this move, Brandon was hired as a social work supervisor at St. Mary's Children's Home. For the next ten years he worked at St. Mary's.

Brandon and Laura joined Reconcilers Fellowship, a bilingual, multi-cultural Mennonite church. About sixty people attended this small house church. It was completely lay-led; there were no paid staff. Pastoral responsibilities rotated between three men, and men and women shared equally in all teaching responsibilities. The community worshipped in English and Spanish, although not everyone was bilingual. Another distinctive mark of this small congregation was its high level of commitment to social ministries. Nearly every member of Reconcilers Fellowship was actively involved in Christian service. Some worked with Habitat for Humanity, others volunteered in after-school tutoring programs for children, several worked at local food banks and homeless shelters, and all of them advocated for peace and non-violence. Many members of this congregation were also active supporters of FFA. This community's sense of compassion and justice for the poor and vulnerable struck a chord with the Dicortes. These Christians with whom Brandon and Laura worshiped and formed community took the radical nature of Christian discipleship very seriously. Their commitment to living the ethics of the Kingdom of God, as Jesus taught in the Sermon on the Mount (Matthew 5-7; cf. Luke 6:17-49), challenged and nurtured Brandon to live a life shaped by the Gospel, rather than to settle for a comfortable form of cultural Christianity. Christian ethics also sustained his commitment to social work practice.

With the birth of their second child, Brandon began considering other employment options. He no longer wanted to be on call 24-hours a day several days a week, as he now was as one of the senior social work administrators for St. Mary's. Brandon wanted more time with his sons and he desperately wanted to work more directly on issues of social justice. Learning of these desires, Pete and several members of FFA's board, some of whom attended Reconcilers Fellowship, approached Brandon about the possibility of assuming some of the agency's administrative, business, and development work in order to free Pete to focus more on training interns and managing operations of the 60-acre farm. Recruiting Brandon, because of his administrative experience at St. Mary's, reflected FFA's organizational growth toward building a more specialized staff. This seemed just the opportunity Brandon had prayed for. He could reduce his workload, spend more time with his wife and children, and work with what he considered to be a unique faith-based organization. Brandon joined the staff in November of 2001 as their first Development Director. Nine months later he found himself in a most uncomfortable predicament.

Louis Touissant

Louis Touissant was a rather large man; he was stocky and nearly six feet tall. His imposing size belied a quiet, gracious, extremely deferential personality. Perhaps his personality had been tempered by the forty-odd years of grinding poverty and inescapable suffering he knew from rural village life in Haiti; perhaps it reflected a combination of cultural deference and his limited English language skills.

Louis arrived at FFA in June of 2001, several months before Brandon joined the staff. Louis, like Brandon, was no stranger to FFA. FFA had worked in the rugged rural landscape of southeastern Haiti, particularly in the village of Petit Jacmel, since 1981. Louis participated in FFA's development work in Jacmel from the very beginning. In 1987, his older brother, Blaise, successfully founded Food for Haiti (FAH), a sister-agency to FFA. FFA and FAH worked closely together to promote agricultural, technical, and educational programs in the village and district of Jacmel. Louis, who had completed agroforestry training at Port-au-Prince's Agricultural Polytechnic Institute, taught basic agroforestry skills and education at FAH's training center. He often expressed an interest in coming to FFA for additional training and education. Because his English skills were far too limited to make him an eligible intern candidate, he enrolled in several English courses in Jacmel. Louis earned high marks in every class and finally achieved his goal—he applied to FFA and was accepted as an intern.

Unfortunately, Louis did not adjust well to life in central Louisiana or as a FFA intern. Being from the tropics, he had great difficulty coping with the cool fall and cold winter weather. And, despite the good grades he earned in his English courses, his language skills proved to be much poorer than anyone expected. As a result, he had a hard time communicating and understanding.

Louis's relationship with the staff and other interns soon became strained when he refused to share in domestic chores that were part of life on the farm and in the dormitory. Although these communal responsibilities had been explained in the application materials, Louis seemed to think that men, particularly educated men like himself, did not participate in preparing or cleaning up after meals, doing dishes, or general cleaning in the dining hall, kitchens, and bathrooms. These tasks belonged to women and children. His attitudes about gender did not entirely surprise the staff at FFA. They had experienced this with other men from developing countries. But, it did create added tensions between Louis and some of the interns, particularly with female interns who Louis expected to do his dormitory chores for him.

Something else, however, did surprise FFA's staff. Louis began talking about going to Christian International Relief and Development (CIRAD), another agricultural development agency located in Sarasota, Florida, for additional training and education. Louis broached this topic with Pete on several occasions. Brandon, whose office was across the hall from Pete's, often overheard these conversations. On a particularly cold day in February, Louis announced he was going to CIRAD and from CIRAD he would return to Petit Jacmel. Pete and Brandon tried, but failed, to convince Louis to finish his internship at FFA. Before Louis departed, Pete and Brandon made it a point to discuss Louis's visa restrictions with him, emphasizing his responsibility to adhere to his August return date. Louis had spent nearly seven months improving his English and they were painfully clear with him on this point. Louis reassured them he would return to Haiti in accordance with his visa.

Once Louis left FFA, Pete and Brandon never heard from him again. Louis never contacted them. He never arrived at CIRAD. He never contacted his brother. He never returned to Haiti.

The board meeting

FFA enjoyed strong support from a deeply committed and very active Board of Directors. The board made decisions and set policy for the agency, and nearly every member was involved with at least one of FFA's projects; most were well-known to the interns and volunteers. The board met every other month and standing committees met between board meetings. FFA's standing committees included Executive, Program, Fundraising and Development, and Public Relations. Pete served as the *ex officio* member of the Executive and Program committees and Brandon was the *ex officio* member on the Fundraising and Development and the Public Relations committees. Although Pete and Brandon were not members of the board, they worked very closely with these committees, submitted staff reports, and were involved, to a large degree, in the agency's decision-making processes.

Everyone at FFA was active in Christian congregations. Ironically, despite their deep faith-commitments, neither the board nor the staff engaged in much 'religious' or 'God-talk.' They shared a common worldview that informed FFA's mission and were committed to working for and alongside the world's poor. Theologically, everyone enjoyed a strong kinship.

Pete, Brandon, and two of the board members worshiped together at Reconcilers Fellowship, three others attended mainline Protestant churches, and the remaining two attended a large interdenominational, urban church known for its service to the urban poor. This contributed significantly to the deep theological and vocational connections shared between staff and board members. Everyone knew one another well enough that the obvious—their commitment to following Christ and the practical implications and application of that commitment—was implicitly a part of their conversations. It rarely needed to be made explicit.

Yet, in spite of all of this, Pete's disclosure to the board that Louis had disappeared elicited a wide-range of strong reactions from board members. "Well, aren't we going to report this to INS?" was one of the first remarks. When Brandon heard it, he became tense and nervous. He foresaw a serious fight brewing.

"I don't think that's appropriate," Pete replied. "It was Louis' responsibility to leave the country, not ours to make sure he left. Even though our name is on the visa, INS does not give us that responsibility. They never say anything like that in any of the paperwork."

"Well, what have we done in the past?" Allen Jeffreys asked. "Has this happened before?" Allen had joined the board the previous year and, although he was still rather new, he had a knack for seeing multiple solutions to vexing problems. This had proven helpful in resolving tough decisions in the past.

Pete and Angela Santos, the board president, exchanged looks, and, after a thoughtful pause, each shook their heads. "No," they both replied in unison.

"This is the first instance in, what, the twenty-something years we've worked with international interns," Angela continued. "I don't believe we have any written policies on this either." Pete's body language indicated she was correct.

"Do you think this will affect future opportunities for getting visas for other applicants, I mean, if INS or someone finds out?" Brenda asked.

Brandon noticed that Allison nodded in agreement. Brenda and Allison were often quick to consider legal and liability issues that might affect the agency.

"I for one think we need a policy to protect ourselves," Jesse Farrar chimed in. Jesse was not on the Board of Directors yet, but his wife, Elizabeth, was and it was a board tradition to invite potential board members to a meeting before issuing them an invitation to join the board. "I don't want this agency to look like a wormhole for illegal immigration. I mean, he basically used us to immigrate, didn't he? Isn't that about right? We can't be seen as somehow encouraging this or as being an easy way for people to come into the country. Do we want to be seen as, 'If you want an easy way into America, try this'?"

"I think it's really easy for people to think that way, Jesse," Brandon intervened. "There's an element of anger we're all feeling over this because that's not why we're here. We're not getting money from donors to run a non-profit organization that trains international interns in sustainable agriculture and then to have them remain here and not return home. I understand some of us being quite upset and wanting to act on that. I just don't know how productive it will be."

"But somehow," Allison stressed, "we've got to write into policy that we will report them if they don't return home. We need to be stronger on this than we are. And if not a policy," she blurted out in near exasperation, "then what?"

"What about our intern screening process?" Allen suggested. "Is there a problem with it? I mean, are there weaknesses in how we recruit and screen potential interns? If some of us are uncomfortable with creating new policies, then perhaps we should consider other things we could do to safeguard ourselves and ensure that international interns do return home—willingly."

"Hey, the screening process can't be that flawed," Percy Manning observed. "I mean, twenty-something years—isn't that what you said, Angela?—and this is the first time this has happened. Maybe this was the exception."

"Or, perhaps we made an error in judging Louis' application," Pete mumbled.

"What do you mean?" a couple people spoke at once.

"We've been successful in not having any international interns go AWOL," Pete began, with a rather dejected sigh, "not because we've been lucky, but because we've always determined that they have sufficient family connections back home to make it as unlikely as possible they would consider staying in the States. Until Louis, this meant that we've only accepted married men, usually fathers, as interns. We've resisted pressure to accept spouses or children because, with their family present, that would make it all the easier for them to decide to stay here and violate their visa."

"And Louis, although he is Blaise's brother and has other brothers and sisters in Jacmel," Angela finished Pete's thought, "was single and had no children."

"Why did we accept him, then?" Jesse asked.

"We thought we knew him well enough. We've known him since we started working in Jacmel, when he was a young man. I saw Louis more as a partner in our work in Haiti than as an international intern. It seemed like a great opportunity for all of us" answered Pete.

"I just can't believe Louis did this!" Elizabeth moaned.

"It's frustrating, I know," Brandon replied, "to face this lost opportunity, but Louis' decision isn't too hard to understand. There are tens of thousands of Haitians living in south Florida; he even has friends from Jacmel living there. It's entirely possible to understand some of what he was thinking and why he did what he did."

"It's completely understandable," Pete said, a bit more energetically. "He got introduced to American culture. He can find a minimum wage job here and make far more than he ever could back in Haiti and he can get involved in Florida's Haitian community. It's all completely rational, what's irrational is going back! So, frankly, I'm rather sympathetic and just don't see any reason we should sic our government on him. I mean, most of us don't even believe immigration should be illegal or restricted from poor, developing countries like Haiti. It boils down to an issue of justice, if you ask me. So, it just doesn't follow that since we're in business because we're called to be compassionate to those who suffer, to help them realize opportunities and create better futures for them and their families and their communities—for people like Louis—that we should be a part of forcing them back into lives of poverty and despair. How can we turn around and, just because Louis chose not to go back to Haiti, start calling the government to hunt this guy down and deport him?"

"I agree," interjected Catherine Kendrick. Catherine was a member of a lay Franciscan order. She had long worked with Christian organizations, both in the U.S. and internationally, on many social justice issues, particularly poverty, hunger, peace and non-violence, and racial reconciliation. She joined the board the previous year, and was already well-respected in the organization. "We're supposed to be people of compassion," she continued. "We are called, over and over again in Scripture, to care for the stranger in our land. I mean it's all over the place. And I don't think we can rationalize having Louis prosecuted for immigrating here and think we are doing what God would have us do. What Louis did may be 'illegal,' but in matters of faith, I think we owe a greater responsibility to honoring God and loving our neighbor."

"Sure, I hear what you're saying, Catherine, but I'm concerned about our liability," Allison replied. "Aren't we liable to the INS? Can't they fine us or get us into trouble? Plus, won't this hurt our chances for getting other interns? And what if word gets out in the community? Do you think people will think twice about supporting us financially if they think we're looking the other way on issues like this? I think we need to be very pro-active about preventing this from happening again."

"But Allison, there's nothing in their literature about us being responsible for this. It rests solely with the international," Pete reiterated.

"So, what you're saying is that we're not *legally* responsible for this in any way?" Percy asked. "Alright, I can live with that, and quite honestly I'm with Catherine on this one, but, perhaps we should consider what we as an agency should do. You know, what is the ethical thing for us to do?"

"Percy has a point," Brandon interjected, "it seems like we need to move from 'We don't have to do anything' to considering, 'What, in good faith, should we do?'"

"Good point, Brandon," Angela remarked. "What do *you* think we should do?"

7

Unanswered Prayers

Mackenzi Huyser

Social worker Stephanie Underwood heard the door close quietly as someone, perhaps another client, entered the office suite.

"Good morning, I'm here for a ten o'clock appointment with Ms. Underwood," Stephanie heard a woman say to the receptionist.

"Welcome to Unity Center, Rebecca. My name is Erica. Please follow me to Stephanie's office," the receptionist responded.

Stephanie straightened a pile of papers on her desk as she heard them walking slowly down the short hall. She thought back to the brief telephone conversation they had yesterday. Rebecca had seemed rushed when they were setting the appointment and had to end the conversation before Stephanie had a chance to complete the initial intake form. Stephanie was surprised she had still shown up for the appointment and wondered what brought this client to her office on a warm summer morning.

Unity Center

Located in Apple Valley, a southern suburb of the Twin Cities (MN), the Unity Center was established to provide a safe haven for women experiencing domestic violence. Established in 1995 as a non-profit organization, the Unity Center was

Development of this decision case was supported in part by the University of South Carolina College of Social Work. It was prepared solely to provide material for class discussion and not to suggest either effective or ineffective handling of the situation depicted. While based on field research regarding an actual situation, names and certain facts may have been disguised to protect confidentiality. The author and editors wish to thank the anonymous case reporter for cooperation in making this account available for the benefit of social work students and practitioners.

Revised from Huyser, M. A. (2003). Unanswered prayers. *Social Work & Christianity, 30*(2), 170-177. Copyright © 2003 NACSW.

a private Christian organization supported by churches and private foundations, as well as United Way-designated funds. Its executive director, with assistance from a board committee, actively solicited these funds to support the agency. A twelve-member board of directors set policy for the Unity Center and hired the executive director. Four board members were official representatives from supporting churches, while others included professionals such as CPAs, attorneys, and community advocates in domestic violence. Board members were selected through open nominations, and participated in an interview process. Board service required a two-year commitment, but could not exceed six years.

The current executive director provided innovative leadership to the agency and had promoted development of additional family support programs. Seven full-time professional staff, with degrees in social work and counseling, provided counseling, family advocacy, and immediate shelter services for more than 100 women and their families each year. Volunteers provided additional services such as cleaning the office, assisting with childcare, and general upkeep of the shelter facilities.

The Unity Center was developed to fill a need for women of faith. For that reason, it maintained a policy of hiring only Christians, and asked job applicants to describe their personal journey of faith during the formal hiring process. The Center also required all staff to be female, in accordance with federal law under the Equal Employment Opportunity Commission.

The Center maintained close relationships with the Christian community through both community education and awareness programs. It also relied on financial support from the Christian community for nearly one-fourth of the annual budget. In particular, ten churches together committed to providing financial support of more than $30,000 each year. In addition to financial support, churches provided numerous volunteers to assist the agency in meeting its mission.

Stephanie Underwood

After finishing her social work field practicum at a domestic violence agency, Stephanie knew she wanted to do that type of work "for the rest of my life." Something inside had just clicked. She especially loved the clients and the tremendous variety of issues they brought. She discovered a passion for promoting human dignity and worth, the idea that human life had value and people should be treated with respect, and for opposing violence against women and children. In short, she believed working in the field of domestic violence allowed her to work for social justice. What's more, she could witness women discovering their potential, developing their gifts, and developing a sense of meaning.

One Saturday morning in May 2000, Stephanie marched down the graduation aisle with her chin held high and shoulders pushed back. Two days later, she began a full time position as a "family advocate" for the Unity Center. She was twenty-two years old, newly married to the man she had dated throughout college, and felt ready to face the world.

Two years later, still "loving every minute" of her job, Stephanie began taking on more responsibilities at the agency. In addition to scheduling initial assessments, making referrals, attending meetings with attorneys for civil and criminal cases, and testifying in court, Stephanie assumed responsibility for developing the agency's community education and awareness programs.

Stephanie believed it was important to educate the community about domestic violence. It was essential to educate people of faith, in churches and schools, that domestic violence did exist, even in Christian homes, and how to support the women involved.

Stephanie's husband supported her career. He could see her passion for the work but had difficulty understanding how she could handle the stress. Their relationship was strong, and Stephanie made her feelings known about many issues in their relationship. She was determined to have equality in their relationship, and had also made him well aware that if he ever threatened her like her clients were threatened, he would be "out the door." Both of their parents had stayed married through "thick and thin," and she was determined to have a successful, happy marriage as well.

Tuesday Morning, 10:00 am

"Good morning, Rebecca," Stephanie said as she met the receptionist and Rebecca just outside her office door. "Please come in and have a seat. May I offer you any coffee, tea, or water?" Stephanie asked out of habit.

"Coffee would be wonderful, thank you," Rebecca responded.

Stephanie excused herself and walked down the hall toward the small kitchen donated by Evergreen Christian Church. It was a generous donation from the large congregation but every time Stephanie entered it she thought of the frail woman who came to see her just three months before. A member of Evergreen for more than 15 years, she had suffered in a violent relationship. *Did her church give her as much emotional support dealing with her relationship as they gave Unity Center in financial support?* Stephanie wondered.

Stephanie filled a mug with coffee, and returned down the hall to the office. She set the coffee on the small table in front of her office window and took a seat across from Rebecca.

"Thank you," Rebecca responded, and took a long deep breath. "I heard about the Unity Center from a friend. I know you provide services to women in violent relationships. I need to know my options."

"Can you tell me the history of your situation?" Stephanie questioned.

In response, Rebecca told how she had married at age 22, believing it would last forever. She had grown up in the church and always thought "marriage was a perfect gift from God." She and her husband, Steve, got pregnant after three years, and nine months later gave birth to a perfect baby boy. Two years later a second boy arrived and their family felt complete.

The early years with the boys were full of fun memories. Rebecca was an accomplished musician, frequently accompanying soloists on the organ and piano. The boys were fond of their mother, watching with amazement as her long fingers moved quickly over the black and white keys each evening. Steve would also, on occasion, join in the practice sessions and smile as his wife played through hymns with such grace and poise.

It was Steve, in fact, who suggested she apply for the open part-time position at church as Assistant Director of Music. Rebecca and Steve were long-time members of Faith Presbyterian Church, a congregation of the Presbyterian Church in America (PCA). They faithfully attended services and felt deeply connected to the community. Because the boys were six and eight years of age, Steve thought it would give her "something to do" besides take care of the home and the family. This had surprised Rebecca because he always seemed to like having her at home to care for the family. He appreciated that she was always available if he needed her to do something during the day. He always wanted the dinner on the table when he arrived home and loved having the house neat and tidy. But he had insisted that she apply for the position, so she did.

When she was offered the position, Rebecca decided it was a perfect fit to join the church staff. Other staff had been impressed with her vision for the music program. She proudly accepted the position and began the following week. But six months after she began the job, Rebecca noticed life at home began to change.

Her husband had become more irritable and short with her when he came home after work.

"One day, out of the blue," Rebecca said, "Steve came home and told me I needed to save all my receipts so he could file them properly. Within a month he had taken the checkbook and credit cards away from me and when I needed money I had to request it in advance."

"Then a few months after that he started to get a little physical. He would push me and sometimes slap me," Rebecca continued, "sometimes when I would come home after a long day at work, he would call me a cheater and liar, because he thought I was having an affair with one of my co-workers," Rebecca paused. "Other days it was like he was so happy to see me and couldn't wait to tell me about his day."

"Have you reported the abuse to anyone?" Stephanie asked.

"I did disclose what was happening in my marriage to my co-workers at the church," Rebecca stated. "Several people told me to pray harder for Steve and our marriage."

"I also told my pastor and he said the Lord can change people," Rebecca continued, "and I believed what my pastor says so I continued to pray."

Stephanie nodded.

"He also said as Christians we are called to work for reconciliation and forgive each other for our wrongdoings," Rebecca said.

"Have you and Steve tried to work toward reconciliation and address these issues?" Stephanie asked.

Rebecca explained that she had made an appointment for counseling at the church, but Steve refused to "show up" for scheduled appointments.

"He would say, 'I hate to see church folks looking at me like there's something wrong with me. There's no problem. If there's a problem, it's all in your head."

Despite these denials, Rebecca wondered whether Steve believed there was no problem because she often heard of him stopping by the church after she had left for the day, just to 'visit' with the staff. She could picture him mocking her and the imaginary problems they were having to the church staff. Although she did not know what, if anything, he said about their relationship, she thought co-workers discounted her reports of abuse in their relationship.

"I continue to pray," Rebecca stated, "but it's been going on over a year and I don't want to continue to live like this. It feels like my life is so up and down. One week he is full of anger, the next week he tells me how much he loves me. I can't deal with this."

Stephanie shared with Rebecca the services available at Unity Center. Rebecca expressed interest in individual counseling and group sessions, but refused to discuss the possibility of a divorce, stating, "My church is very conservative and believes divorce is not part of God's plan for our lives. I made a commitment to stay with him through good times and bad. God forgives us. Shouldn't I do that for Steve?" Rebecca asked.

"I think that's a decision you need to make for yourself," Stephanie said.

Rebecca nodded hesitantly.

"You can explore these questions in the individual counseling and group sessions if you like," Stephanie suggested.

"Oh, I think that sounds good," Rebecca replied.

"Okay," Stephanie encouraged, "let's get some sessions set up for you first thing next week. Does that sound like it will work?"

"That sounds great."

Stephanie offered some appointment times, and Rebecca selected an individual counseling session for the following Tuesday.

"If you have any emergencies before your appointment," Stephanie explained, "you can call the agency pager and someone will return your call right away."

As she watched Rebecca walk out the door and down the hall, Stephanie felt uneasy wondering how frightening it must be to have the one you love and live with be so volatile.

Tuesday Evening, 6:27 pm

That evening, Stephanie's pager went off in the middle of dinner with her husband. At the moment, they were disagreeing about whether to spend summer vacations with their families. Though disagreements were usually "short and sweet" during their first years of marriage, Stephanie was relieved to have an excuse to leave the table. She didn't recognize the number displayed on the pager but called immediately.

"Stephanie?" the panicked voice on the other line questioned.

"This is Stephanie," she confirmed.

"This is Rebecca. We met this morning in your office. I'm sorry to call you now, the boys are with me and I am driving. He is really starting to scare me. He said he was planning to use his guns soon. I can't stay there."

When the call began to break up, Stephanie asked, "Are you there, Rebecca?"

"Yes," Rebecca answered. "I'm leaving. I can't take this."

"I can get you into our shelter program tonight. That will be a safe place for you to stay until we can file the paperwork for a Petition for Relief. A petition will ensure he is put out of the home."

"I'm on my way to my sister's house. We'll be safe there tonight," Rebecca stated. "Can we meet first thing in the morning to file for a Petition?"

"OK, let's meet at the office at eight o'clock," Stephanie suggested. "Be careful."

Wednesday Morning

The next morning, as Rebecca made her way down the hall to Stephanie's office, she appeared fatigued, even discouraged. Stephanie commented gently, "You look pretty tired."

"I had trouble sleeping last night," Rebecca explained, "but I know I need to take these steps to make myself and my boys safe."

Stephanie asked Rebecca to describe what had happened since their previous conversation.

"Last night I went out to the garage to call my husband for dinner," Rebecca began. "He was bent over his workbench and when I walked in he looked up at me with this frightening look in his eyes."

Rebecca began to shake as she described "the look."

"He was cleaning his handguns," Rebecca paused.

Stephanie nodded, urging Rebecca to continue.

"When I saw that, I panicked," Rebecca said, "just grabbed the boys and left for my sister's house."

Stephanie nodded again.

"I called you from the road," Rebecca said, looking down at the floor and pausing. "I knew," Rebecca started and then took a deep breath, "I knew, at that moment our relationship was over, that it had to end. It had just reached a new level."

Stephanie shook her head, indicating she understood. She went on to explain that, depending on what the court decided, the Petition for Relief could restrain her husband from committing acts of domestic violence by keeping him from their home and from an appropriate area surrounding their home and her workplace. But Rebecca did not seem satisfied.

Stephanie paused, wondering whether she should recommend Rebecca also file for divorce. It certainly seemed that Rebecca wanted to take this to the next level, but Stephanie always felt some pain in suggesting it. Hesitantly, she continued, "We could also file a Marriage Dissolution Petition. You will have six months before the divorce is finalized so you can still work toward reconciliation."

"I think we should file for both," Rebecca responded without hesitating.

As the women worked to complete the two petitions, Stephanie asked, "In the meantime, how will you stay safe?"

"I am going to stay at my sister's house through next week until I can figure out what this all means," Rebecca stated. "My boys and I feel safe there, and my sister can help me think through this mess."

"Can we meet again next Wednesday to see where you are with things?" Stephanie questioned.

"Yes, I think that will work out fine," Rebecca said.

"If you need anything, anything at all, call me," Stephanie said as she walked Rebecca to the door, "Take care and I will see you next week," Stephanie concluded.

Monday Afternoon

Five days later, when Stephanie returned from lunch, Erica informed her Rebecca had called and left a message on her voicemail. Stephanie listened to the message immediately.

"Stephanie, this is Rebecca," her voice shaking with apparent anger. "My husband told our pastor I filed for divorce and the elders called me in and told me to drop the divorce because it is something we need to work out together through the church and that divorce is not part of God's plan for our lives. They said they should be the ones to 'help make those decisions' and they want to help us get back together. I told them I had prayed about this and nothing had changed. I finally decided I needed to file this paperwork with you for my own safety and the safety of my children and that I refused to withdraw it. They said my 'lack of cooperation' required church discipline and suspended my membership status. Because I am no longer a member, I was fired from my job. I am on my way to see you. I need to talk about this situation."

As Stephanie replayed the message a second time, she looked toward the parking lot. Rebecca was pulling into an open spot right outside the main door. In a matter of minutes she would be in Stephanie's office looking for help with her situation.

8

BIRTHFATHER'S RIGHT?

Jennifer L. Fahy

"Yeah, this is Jamal Pinckney, Keisha's ex. I got your messages and I don't like this adoption thing." He sounded upset. "I don't believe in adoption, you know. African Americans just don't do adoption. We take care of our own. I wasn't ever gonna have a child of mine be adopted."

"I've been trying to get a hold of you for several months," social worker Gretchen Fuller interrupted. Gretchen's heart sank as she tried to absorb what Jamal was saying.

"Well," Jamal quipped, "I've been busy."

"I can understand that you have a busy life," Gretchen tried to stay calm. "However, time has been passing and Keisha had to look at what was the best option for her and this pregnancy without hearing from you. She considered her options and decided on adoption. Do you have another option for this child?"

"Well," Jamal replied, "I can't take care of it. I'm not even sure it's my child."

Moments later, Jamal ended the conversation almost as abruptly as he began it. As she hung up the phone, Gretchen began to review her options. As the social work supervisor at Trinity Family Services, she knew there weren't many.

Trinity Family Services

Trinity Family Services was a not-for-profit, pro-life, Christian adoption and

Development of this decision case was supported in part by the University of South Carolina College of Social Work. It was prepared solely to provide material for class discussion and not to suggest either effective or ineffective handling of the situation depicted. While based on field research regarding an actual situation, names and certain facts may have been disguised to protect confidentiality. The author and editors wish to thank the anonymous case reporter for cooperation in making this account available for the benefit of social work students and practitioners.

family services agency with offices in several states. In Ohio, Trinity Family Services had offices in Toledo, Cleveland, Cincinnati, and Columbus. Programs included a domestic infant adoption program, international adoption, special needs adoption, crisis pregnancy counseling services, and an abstinence education program. Through these programs, Trinity Family Services worked toward their mission of showing God's love by providing services to improve the lives of children and families. Overall, in the state of Ohio, Trinity Family Services completed about 30 domestic adoptions and 75 international adoptions per year.

Infant Domestic Adoption Program

The infant domestic adoption program at Trinity Family Services in Ohio rarely had to advertise its services. On average, there were about 25 families statewide waiting to adopt an infant at any time. All adoptive children were less than 2 years of age. Trinity Family Services required all prospective adoptive families to be active Christian couples who had been married a minimum of 2 years. These requirements for prospective adoptive families fulfilled Trinity's Christian values of providing stable, married, two-parent homes for children. It usually took approximately 18 months to adopt an infant.

Prospective adoptive families had to complete a series of steps in order to be approved for an adoption. First, prospective adoptive parents completed a written application. Next, one of Trinity's adoption social workers conducted a family assessment which included checking personal and employer references, a background check, family physicals, family and individual interviews, and a home visit. Finally, prospective adoptive parents had to become licensed as foster parents because the adoptive child would live in their home under agency supervision for 6 months before the adoption was finalized. The total cost of the adoption process for families was approximately $13,000. Many of the adoptive families had chosen adoption after years of struggling with infertility. The adoption process for families was often emotional and stressful.

Trinity's infant domestic adoption program funding came largely from fees for services paid by adoptive families subsidized with gifts received from individuals, churches, corporations, and foundations. The total cost of each adoption was about $15,000-16,000.

Gretchen Fuller

Gretchen Fuller, a 25-year-old Caucasian from the Midwest, was in her first so-cial work position at Trinity Family Services in Ohio. Gretchen's Christian world-view and interest in helping children and families drew her to the social work profession. She had always had a particular interest in adoption. Growing up, she had several adopted cousins, and from a young age knew about adoption.

Gretchen attended Rochester College, a small Christian liberal arts school in Michigan, where she majored in sociology. During college, she completed an in-ternship in the pediatric unit of a hospital and really enjoyed working with chil-dren and families. Immediately after graduation, Gretchen entered the University of Michigan's master's program in social work. Gretchen focused on administra-tion and management but balanced her coursework with clinical classes on family systems. During her master's program, Gretchen completed clinical internships at a domestic violence agency and a community mental health agency, and an ad-ministrative placement in a BSW program at a Christian college. After graduation, Gretchen was excited to be hired as a supervisor for Trinity Family Services' Co-lumbus and Cincinnati offices. Gretchen was particularly excited about working in a Christian adoption agency because it allowed her to serve God by helping the "needy, widow, and the orphan" of modern day society.

Gretchen's new position entailed managing eleven staff: five social workers and two support staff in the Cincinnati office and four social workers in the Co-lumbus office. Gretchen's new position required that she re-locate to Cincinnati and travel frequently between the Cincinnati and Columbus sites. Beyond super-vising direct service staff, Gretchen was also in charge of hiring and training new workers, doing budgeting and bill-payment, handling crises any time of the day or night, and taking overflow cases as needed.

Monday, December 27, 2004

As Gretchen walked into her office on a cold December morning she noticed her phone light blinking. She set down her things and pulled her chair up to her desk. She sighed, thinking, *that Christmas holiday was way too short...I'm just not ready for another 60-hour work week. I've only been in this job for 7 months and already I'm burnt out. I wish I could find someone to hire for our open birthparent counselor position to take the pressure off of me.* She picked up the phone and dialed into her voice mail.

"Gretchen, Cindy Novak from Cincinnati Women's Reformatory. It's Thursday, December 23, 4:30 pm. Give me a call."

After listening to her other messages, Gretchen hung up and pulled out Cindy's card from her contact file. *I will have to take this case myself,* she thought, *until I can get a new staff person hired.*

Gretchen had first met Cindy, a social worker at Cincinnati Women's Reformatory, at a workshop last July. Since then she had worked with her on a number of referrals. She picked up the phone and dialed Cindy's direct line.

"Cindy Novak," the voice on the other end said immediately.

"Cindy, this is Gretchen from Trinity Family Services. Just got your message."

"Hey, Gretchen, thanks for calling me back. We just got a new inmate on the segregation unit. She's pregnant and says she is interested in adoption. Can we set up a visit?" Cindy asked.

"Sure," Gretchen said, opening her planner. "I can do tomorrow or Wednesday."

"I can probably get you cleared for Wednesday. How does 9 a.m. work?" Cindy asked.

"Fine, see you then," Gretchen replied.

Wednesday, December 29, 2004

As Gretchen drove across town to the prison for her appointment, she thought about her first experience seeing a prospective birthmother at the prison. *It's a challenge to empower birthparents to make the best decision for themselves in such a restricted environment. They can't make a phone call when they want, schedule their own visits, or even have private conversations. How can I empower this client? Especially when she is in the maximum security segregation unit?*

After parking, Gretchen proceeded straight to the guardhouse. "Hi, I'm Gretchen Fuller. Cindy Novak scheduled an appointment for me to see Keisha Brown."

"Ok, let me check the schedule," the guard said. "I will need to see your driver's license."

"Here you go," said Gretchen. The guard walked back to the office and returned a minute later.

"Alright, here is your visitor's badge; you must have it visible at all times. Why don't you take a moment to lock up any valuables you have in the locker to your right? Here is the key for number 6. It would be best if you removed all your jewelry," the guard directed. "When you've finished come back to the desk and I will take you through the metal detectors."

When Gretchen returned to the desk, the guard directed, "Okay, please step through the metal detector." Gretchen walked through the detector.

"Alright, if you'll wait outside, a guard will be around in a few minutes to pick you up and take you to the maximum security area for your visit."

After a few minutes, a truck pulled up to the guardhouse.

"Hey, Gretchen, long time no see," Joe Mankowski, a long-time guard at the prison, greeted her warmly. "Hop in."

"Hi, Joe! How have you been?" Gretchen asked as they drove off. "Did you have a good Christmas?"

"Yeah, we went to the in-laws' house," Joe replied as he drove to the prison complex. "The kids had a great time. How 'bout you?"

"It was good, nice to relax for a few days, too bad it didn't last longer," Gretchen said as the truck pulled to a stop.

"OK, here we are. Just follow me," Joe directed as they entered a large building. Joe approached a door and unlocked it. "Just wait here, and I'll bring the inmate into the next room in a few minutes."

Gretchen scanned the room. One wall was transparent glass. On the other side of the glass was a room that was a mirror image of the room she was in. Each room had four partitioned booths with a table, chair, and a callbox. She sat in the first booth closest to the door. Gretchen leafed through the information she had brought. After about 20 minutes of waiting, she heard a door open and looked up.

The first person through the door was a young, thin, African-American woman dressed in an oversized orange jumpsuit that almost concealed the small bump on her belly. Her hands were shackled in front of her and her feet were shackled as well. Joe followed her into the room, directed her to sit down, and locked her hand shackles to the table.

The young woman looked up and smiled self-consciously. She leaned her head to her shoulder, "Sorry about my hair. I haven't been able to fix it since I got here."

"I don't imagine they let you have your hair supplies here, huh?" Gretchen said, hoping to break the ice.

"No, they sure don't," Keisha replied with another smile.

"Well, I'm Gretchen Fuller."

"Keisha Brown. I'm glad they let you come over."

"Yeah, Cindy arranged for me to come," Gretchen explained. "She told me that you're interested in adoption."

"That's right," Keisha agreed.

"Well, I would be happy to answer any questions you have about the adoption process. How many months pregnant are you?"

"About six," Keisha answered.

"And I suppose that you'll still be in here when you are due?" Gretchen asked tentatively.

"Yeah, I have a year 'til I'm even up for parole," Keisha explained. "They moved me from Cleveland to the segregation unit here because I walked off from my mandated work release program last summer. So now, I am considered an escapee. Me, an escapee? Yeah, right."

"So, you got pregnant this past summer?" Gretchen asked.

"I was living with my family in Cleveland and I started dating Jamal. Towards the end of the summer, I hadn't gotten my period and wondered if I was pregnant. Sure enough, I was. I told Jamal and he got mad and said he didn't want anything to do with that. Then, the cops found out where I had been living and came over and picked me up," Keisha said.

"I'm not trying to be offensive, but I need to know, are you sure that Jamal is the father?" Gretchen asked.

"Yep," Keisha replied, "he is absolutely the father."

"Do you have any family members," Gretchen explored, "who could help you with the baby?"

"Not really," Keisha said, "only my grandmother and she's already taking care of my son, Devontae. She can't take care of another baby. I don't really have any other options."

I don't like to hear that she doesn't have any options, Gretchen thought. *Adoption is a big choice and it would be better if she felt it was the best choice, not the only option.*

"Is this really what you want to do," Gretchen delved deeper, "or is it just your last option?"

"Well, it is my last option," Keisha shrugged, "but it would also be better for the child. I can't keep this baby 'cause I'm in prison. Jamal hasn't answered any of my letters since I've been here. My grandmother can't handle another child. I've already screwed up by being away from my son and I don't want that for this child."

"It must be really hard to be separated from your son," Gretchen said.

"Yeah, and I don't want this child to have what my son has had. His father doesn't talk to him or take any responsibility. I was raised by my grandmother and didn't really see my mother or father. I just don't want that for another one of my kids."

"You said that Jamal hasn't been talking to you?" Gretchen probed.

"No, Jamal is such a jerk! He hasn't made any attempt to talk to me even though I've been trying to get a hold of him for weeks. He is not taking any responsibility for this."

"Just so you know," Gretchen explained, "in order to complete an adoption, I will need to make a good faith effort to get Jamal's consent to terminate his parental rights."

"Good luck with that," Keisha said sarcastically.

"Well," Gretchen said, "let me tell you a little about my agency and the adoption process. As you know, I work for Trinity Family Services' infant domestic adoption program. We are a not-for-profit, Christian agency and we help birthparents to find good homes for their babies. All of our adoptive families are Christian couples who are married and have been educated about adoption. If you choose adoption, you would fill out some paperwork, choose an adoptive family, and after the baby is born, go to court and explain to a judge that you want to voluntarily terminate your parental rights. This is a very difficult decision and I want you to know that you can change your mind at any time until you terminate your parental rights in court. If you are still interested, I will leave you some information and you can think about it."

"Yeah, I'm still interested," Keisha replied. "Leave me that information and I will think it over."

"This is a very important decision," Gretchen said, "so think about this carefully. If you have any more questions, just tell Cindy and she'll get a hold of me."

"Ok, thanks," Keisha said. "Well, nice to meet ya."

"It was nice to meet you too," Gretchen said.

I wonder if this case will go any further, Gretchen thought as Joe escorted her out of the prison. *A lot of times the first meeting is purely informational and we never hear from the woman again. Nothing is ever certain in an adoption – so many women change their minds. But it's sure encouraging that a woman in such difficult circumstances would choose to carry her baby to term.*

Monday, January 3, 2005

The following Monday, just as Gretchen returned to her desk after leading the weekly staff meeting, her phone rang.

Cindy Novak was on the line. "Keisha Brown is still interested in adoption and she wants to take the next steps."

"Well, the next step for Keisha will be to fill out a pile of paperwork. What would be the best way to do that?" Gretchen asked.

"Keisha can't have a pen in her cell," Cindy explained, "so the best thing would be to have her come up to the social work department where she could work at a desk."

"Okay," Gretchen said. "It's best to have someone available to help with the paperwork as she fills it out. If I am available via phone, could you sit with her in the office while she does the paperwork?"

"Yes, that would be fine. When could you do this?" Cindy asked.

"Well, is there any way you could make time today?" Gretchen asked.

"I could make that work," Cindy said. "Why don't you fax the information over and I will call you back in an hour when I can get Keisha up to the office."

"Okay," Gretchen replied, "I'll wait for your call."

As planned, Keisha filled out the necessary paperwork that afternoon.

Friday, January 21, 2005

A few weeks later, Gretchen returned to the prison to talk with Keisha about her preferences for an adoptive family.

"How are you doing?" Gretchen questioned.

"Okay," Keisha said. "Oh, I found out that I'm having a girl."

"Really?" Gretchen replied. "That's great. By the way, I wanted to let you know that I have sent several letters and left many phone messages for Jamal and he has not contacted me. So as far as we know, we can keep moving forward with this adoption."

"He isn't answering my letters either," Keisha fumed. "He thinks because I'm in jail that he doesn't have to talk to me."

"Well, I'm here today to talk about the things that you want in an adoptive family. What kinds of things are important to you?" Gretchen asked.

"It'd be nice if they were African American," Keisha replied. "But if they're white, then they need to expose the baby to African American culture."

"Good, what else?" Gretchen asked.

"Well, the mom and dad have to be good people. If would be nice if they had other kids for the baby to play with. And now that I know I am having a girl, they have to know how to do hair," Keisha answered. Gretchen and Keisha continued to talk about Keisha's hopes over the next half hour.

As Gretchen left the meeting, she tried to think of a family that would be a good match. *I'll have to check if we have any African American families looking to adopt right now. I know there are several White families available. I wonder if any are open to an African American child,* she thought.

Friday, February 4, 2005

Gretchen answered her phone and heard Amy McDonnell, an adoption social worker in Trinity's Toledo office on the other end of the line.

"Hi, Gretchen! Guess what? Good news. I know you've been looking for an adoptive family for Keisha for two weeks now. Well, I think I found a family she would like. I was at adoption worker training and ran into Beth, an adoption worker from St. Mary's Social Services. She has a family licensed through their minority adoption program and they are looking for a baby to adopt."

"Really? What do you know about them?" Gretchen asked.

"Well, the parents are both Caucasian but they have African American relatives. They live in Toledo and they previously adopted a biracial boy from us. They are both active in the adoption community and have taken classes on cross-racial adoption. We could do an interagency contract with St. Mary's."

"Can you send me their file?" Gretchen asked.

"Absolutely. I hope it works out," Amy replied.

"Me, too," Gretchen answered. After Gretchen received the information on the adoptive family, she looked it over. Thinking this family would be a good match, she mailed the profile to Keisha and crossed her fingers.

Tuesday, February 8, 2005

A few days later, Cindy called to say that Keisha wanted to set up an appointment.

Gretchen was excited and nervous as she drove to the prison for the meeting. *I wonder how she feels about the adoptive family.*

After exchanging greetings, Keisha got straight to the point. "The family looks great, when can I meet them?"

"Well," Gretchen replied, "I can give them a call when I get back to the office and set up an appointment."

"Good. I want to get all this stuff settled," Keisha said.

When Gretchen got back to the office, she immediately called the adoptive family. Evelyn Anderson answered the phone, "Hello?"

"Hi, my name is Gretchen Fuller. I am a birthparent counselor at Trinity Family Services. I believe that Amy McDonnell, an adoption social worker here at Trinity spoke with you and your caseworker from St. Mary's about a birthmother we are working with who is interested in adoption. I showed her your profile and she's interested in meeting you both. How do you feel about coming to the Cincinnati Women's Reformatory to meet her?"

"Sure, it takes about ninety minutes to drive there. When are you thinking?" Evelyn asked.

"I have spoken with the social worker at the prison and she said that Tuesday, February 22, at 2 p.m. would be a good meeting time. Would that work for you and your husband?" Gretchen asked.

"Let me check my calendar," Evelyn replied. A moment later, she said, "Yes that would be fine."

Tuesday, February 22, 2005

The Andersons met Gretchen at the Cincinnati office to drive together to the prison.

"How are you feeling about our meeting today?" Gretchen asked as they left for the prison.

"We're really excited, Evelyn said. "I hope she likes us."

"I hope so too," Gretchen responded.

"Do you know of any complications with this case, Gretchen?" Ken asked. "When we adopted our first child we had a number of issues with the birthfather agreeing to the adoption. It was very stressful and the adoption almost didn't go through."

"Well, so far," Gretchen explained, "after repeated attempts, we haven't heard from the father. The birthmother, Keisha, is certain that she wants to do this adoption. Today, we will be meeting with her over a videoconference system. She's in the maximum security division and normally wouldn't be allowed any visitors, but the prison has allowed these special meeting arrangements due to Keisha's circumstances."

"When is Keisha due?" Evelyn asked.

"In just one week. Well, here we are. We'll have to go through security checks once we're inside," Gretchen added.

After going through all the checks and screening, the Andersons accompanied Gretchen to the visitor meeting area. A guard showed them to a small partitioned area in the room with a TV, camera, and phone box. They pulled three chairs over and soon realized that the camera could only see one person at a time. To talk to Keisha, they had to take turns with the phone and the chair placed directly in front of the camera. Fortunately, the Andersons seemed to find musical chairs more humorous than frustrating. Keisha asked them all sorts of questions, including if they knew how to do African American girls' hair. Evelyn assured her that she knew it was very important for little girls' hair to be perfect.

Later that day, Cindy called Gretchen to report, "Keisha said the family is good. Go ahead and set it up."

Great, Gretchen thought, *everything is falling into place. Keisha likes the Andersons and the baby will have a good Christian home to grow up in.* Gretchen called the court office and was able to squeeze onto the court schedule a termination of parental rights hearing for March 25th.

Thursday, March 3, 2005

"This is Gretchen Fuller," Gretchen answered as she answered the phone.

"Yeah, this is Jamal Pinkney, Keisha's ex. I got your messages and I don't like this adoption thing. Is this really what Keisha wants? I mean, doesn't she have someone who can take care of this baby?" Jamal sounded upset. "I don't believe in adoption, you know. African Americans just don't do adoption. We take care of our own. I wasn't ever gonna have a child of mine be adopted."

"I've been trying to get a hold of you for several months," Gretchen interrupted. Her heart sank as she tried to absorb what Jamal was saying.

"Well," Jamal quipped, "I've been busy."

"I can understand that you have a busy life," Gretchen tried to stay calm. "However, time has been passing and Keisha had to look at what was the best option for her and this pregnancy without hearing from you. She considered her options and decided on adoption. Do you have another option for this child?"

"Well," Jamal replied, "I can't take care of it. I'm not even sure it's my child."

"Keisha named you as the only possible birthfather." Gretchen answered.

"Whatever, that doesn't make it my child. But," Jamal continued, "I still don't know about this adoption thing. African Americans don't just give their children away."

"I think that she's just looking for the best possible plan for this child's future," Gretchen replied. "She loves this child very much and this is a difficult decision for her."

"I need to think about it. I gotta go," Jamal said as he hung up the phone.

Monday, March 7, 2005

On Monday morning, Gretchen checked her messages after being out of town for the weekend. The baby had been born in the hospital on Saturday afternoon and Keisha had already been transported back to prison Sunday morning. They needed someone to fill out all the discharge papers and pick up the child.

Gretchen got straight to work. She faxed back and forth the necessary paperwork to the jail and hospital. By mid-day, she had a foster parent from Trinity's receiving home program pick up the baby. It was Trinity's policy to place the baby in a temporary foster receiving home until the court date to terminate parental rights. Then, the baby would be transferred to the pre-adoptive home.

After settling matters, she called Keisha to check up on her. "Hi Keisha, how are you feeling?"

"I'm feeling okay. I'm pretty tired. I'm having a really bad day today. I finally got a letter back from that jerk, Jamal," Keisha complained angrily. "He waits all this time to write me and now he thinks he gets to tell me what to do!"

"What did the letter say?" Gretchen asked.

"He wrote that what I'm doing is wrong and he doesn't think he is the father. He said even if he was the father, he wouldn't agree to this adoption and that I need to find someone to take care of this child. Of course," Keisha fumed, "he's not offering any help. I don't have any relatives to take care of this baby, but he wouldn't know that because he never talked to me. Just sends me a letter out of nowhere!"

"On top of everything," Keisha stated, "I called my grandmother today and told her I had a baby."

"You hadn't told her you were pregnant?" Gretchen asked incredulously.

"Actually, no. She was really upset. She was against the adoption, too. She said she definitely couldn't take care of another child. She said that maybe I should let the child go into the foster care system in Cleveland and then someday I could get her back. But I'm not sure that is a good idea. I don't want this child to go through moving from house to house and not knowing any family. I don't know that I would ever get the baby back for sure anyways, and this way I know that she will have a good, stable family that I have chosen."

"Well, as you know, it is still not too late to make another decision. Until you terminate your parental rights at court, you can make any decision you feel is best. You should also be aware that the state has the right to terminate your parental rights involuntarily once the child is in the foster care system. What would you like me do at this point?" Gretchen asked. "Or do you need more time to think about it?"

"I've already thought about it enough," Keisha said. "I still want to go forward with the adoption. It's the best option I have. I'll talk to my grandmother and Jamal again and explain to them why I am doing this."

Tuesday, March 8, 2005 – Friday, March 18, 2005

For the next several weeks, Gretchen was inundated with calls. Keisha's grandmother, Josephine, called her on several occasions, always saying the same thing. "I don't believe in adoption. This is wrong. I can't take this child but I am going to find a relative who can." However, after repeated calls to relatives, Josephine couldn't find anyone to care for the baby and did not want to take care of the baby herself.

Gretchen also received a phone call nearly every other day from Jamal. At first, he kept expressing that he could not be the father. He wanted a DNA test. So Gretchen set up a test for him. A week before the test, his attitude changed.

"I just want to find out if I'm the father," he said. "I think she's a liar."

"If you are the father," Gretchen asked, "then what are you going to do?"

"Even if I am the father," Jamal replied, "I can't take care of this child. So I guess we're going to have to do this adoption thing."

A week later, the test results confirmed Jamal's paternity. He and Gretchen set up a time to sign paperwork terminating his parental rights.

Monday, March 21, 2005

Gretchen drove across the state to the Trinity Family Services' Cleveland office to meet Jamal. When he came in, she immediately recognized that the baby had his facial features. Gretchen began explaining the paperwork to him, careful to make sure he understood everything he was signing. He signed the notice of the court hearing on March 25th and his right to appear. He signed the most important document--the consent to terminate parental rights--and the notice that he had received a copy of Ohio adoption laws. Gretchen got to the last form, which was by far the longest and most complex. It was Trinity's legal document for birthfathers, *Your Alternatives and Rights*. The form explained all the birthfather's rights and informed him of possible alternatives to giving up parental rights.

Suddenly, Jamal sat back and folded his arms, "I'm not ready to sign that."

"Okay," Gretchen replied, "that's fine. However, I want you to know that this form is not a necessary form, only a supplement. You don't have to sign it and your rights can still be terminated."

"I just can't sign that now," Jamal seemed upset. He shifted several times in his seat and began looking around the room.

After a few more minutes of conversation, Gretchen gave Jamal copies of all the forms and he left.

On her drive home, Gretchen kept thinking, *What happened? He was filling out the paperwork and then all of a sudden he stopped. He didn't take back the papers he had already signed. Maybe the language of the last document made him change his mind? Then why didn't he ask for the other papers to be torn up?*

Tuesday, March 22, 2005

The next day Jamal called Gretchen. He asked, "Do I still need to sign that last form?"

Again, Gretchen explained that it was not needed; she could present the documents he had already signed. That would be sufficient for terminating his parental rights.

"I just wish I could talk to her on the phone," Jamal said. "You know, I can't talk to her in segregation, only send her letters. I'd feel better about all this if I could talk to her."

"Let me see if I can arrange a phone call," Gretchen said. "I'll get back to you as soon as I know."

Gretchen called Cindy at the prison to see if there was any way that Keisha could make a phone call to Jamal. Cindy's supervisor approved it so they set up a call for a couple days later.

Thursday, March 24, 2005

It was now only one day before the scheduled court date. Gretchen traveled to the prison to be there when Keisha made the call. After Gretchen finished prepping Keisha for court, Keisha dialed Jamal. *Hopefully, this call will resolve this,* Gretchen thought.

But the call did not go well. Jamal screamed at Keisha, telling her that it was her fault she was in prison and her fault that this baby had nowhere to go. Keisha was both crying and angry. She explained why she thought adoption was the best option to Jamal. However, at the end of the thirty-minute phone call there was still no resolution.

After she had hung up the phone, Keisha was very angry, "He's just messing with me. He wants to get back at me. He doesn't care about what is best for the baby."

That afternoon, when Gretchen got back to her office, Jamal called her again. His thoughts and sentences were scattered. He asked, "What's going to happen now?"

"Well," Gretchen said, "Keisha still wants to do this adoption. She's ready to terminate her parental rights at court tomorrow. As far as I can tell, you understand the termination of parental rights paperwork we filled out and that you have a right to appear at court tomorrow. You haven't said that you have a different plan for the baby, so the case is still proceeding."

"I'm the father of this baby," Jamal interrupted, "I don't think I can do this adoption. I don't know. I'm just not sure." He rambled on for several minutes sounding conflicted and confused until he abruptly stated, "I gotta go. I'll call you later."

After Jamal had hung up, Gretchen thought about her options. *What should I do? The baby has to go somewhere. Keisha clearly wants the child to be adopted, and Jamal has no alternative to offer. The court hearing is set for tomorrow.*

9

THE MENTAL HEALTH AND SPIRITUALITY WORKSHOP

Carrie Yocum and Terry A. Wolfer

As a rehab practitioner in the Intensive Psychiatric Rehabilitation Treatment Program at Albany Community Mental Health Center, Kolap White had designed a Mental Health and Spirituality Workshop, an optional 12-week series of interactive group sessions for program clients. During the seventh week, Cathy Crider, a client who had shown much interest in previous sessions, arrived late and remained quiet throughout the session.

After the session ended and other group members had left, Kolap approached her tentatively. "Are you okay? You seem upset."

"Kolap," Cathy exclaimed quietly, "I don't mean to be rude, but I hate this workshop!"

Albany, New York

Although Albany had a population of barely 100,000 people, it exerted unusual influence as the seat of New York state government and the home of the State University of New York-Albany campus. With a population of nearly 300,000, Albany County was also the major population center between New York City and the Ad-

Development of this decision case was supported in part by the University of South Carolina College of Social Work. It was prepared solely to provide material for class discussion and not to suggest either effective or ineffective handling of the situation depicted. While based on field research regarding an actual situation, names and certain facts may have been disguised to protect confidentiality. The authors and editors wish to thank the anonymous case reporter for cooperation in making this account available for the benefit of social work students and practitioners.

Revised from Yocum, C. (2003). The mental health and spirituality workshop. *Social Work & Christianity*, 30(2), 149-161. Copyright © 2003 NACSW.

irondack Mountains. The county was predominantly Caucasian, though African Americans comprised 26% of its population.

Albany Community Mental Health Center

The mission of the Albany Community Mental Health Center (ACMHC) was to improve the quality of life of people with mental illnesses. To accomplish this, AC-MHC offered a wide array of counseling, educational, housing, and support services for people of all ages and backgrounds. These services included crisis services, adult general psychiatric services, gero-psychiatric services, psychiatric group home, case management, children and youth services, drug and alcohol services, psychosocial rehabilitation, and intensive psychiatric rehabilitation. As a large public agency, ACMHC employed nearly 70 rehab practitioners, outpatient therapists, and other health care professionals, and 10 administrative staff members.

Intensive Psychiatric Rehabilitation Treatment

Among the many programs at ACMHC was the Intensive Psychiatric Rehabilitation Treatment Program (IPRT). IPRT aimed to help consumers—their preferred designation for program participants—improve their environmental supports, overcome functional disabilities, and achieve and maintain desired roles in life. It assisted consumers in forming and achieving goals in their living, learning, working and social environments. It focused on improving their functioning in specific settings while simultaneously respecting personal choice, satisfaction, and self-determination. Typically, IPRT consumers participated in groups five hours per day, three days per week. They usually spent six months to two years in the program, depending on how rapidly they achieved their goals.

IPRT Referral and Intake

Most referrals came from within the county and more than eighty percent of the program consumers were Medicaid recipients. IPRT served only adults diagnosed with mental illness, typically with a primary psychiatric diagnosis of Depression, Bipolar, Schizophrenia, or drug and alcohol problems. Consumers received ongoing psychiatric treatment to stabilize their symptoms. Consumers also had functional deficits that were expected to last one year or more, in achieving and/or maintaining desired living, learning, working, or social roles or environments. Many had low tolerance for everyday stressors such as conflict with significant others, bosses or co-workers, or managing and paying their bills.

Consumers in this program had expressed dissatisfaction with their situations or had struggled to meet the demands of their various life roles. They had also expressed the desire and motivation to make changes in their lives.

Upon acceptance into the program, consumers were assigned an outpatient therapist in addition to a rehab practitioner. Agency policy required that a consumer's outpatient therapist—not the rehab practitioner—address "therapy issues."

IPRT Services

The IPRT Program consisted of phase groups and workshops. In the phase groups, rehab practitioners worked with consumers to develop individualized service plans that outlined the skills they needed, how they would learn those skills, and who would provide services and support. Individual consumers decided on the goal, the pathway, and the pace. Consumers chose a goal in the first phase, achieved it in the second, and worked to maintain it in the third. The phase groups consisted of curricula that facilitated consumers' achievement of their goals and movement through the phases.

Simultaneously, consumers typically participated in a variety of workshops. They selected these workshops based on personal needs, as suggested by their rehab practitioner, or personal interests. The workshops focused on skill-building with topics such as anger management, self-esteem and confidence, positive thinking, creative healing, computer practice, goal setting, mental health and wellness, and educational or vocational needs. The workshops were conducted once per week and usually lasted for three months. Though averaging seven members, workshops were comprised of three to fifteen people and were open to new members throughout the three months unless they became too large to accommodate new members. Consumers were encouraged to take at least five skill-building workshops to assist them in reaching their goals.

All rehab practitioners conducted five workshops per week, but had considerable autonomy in choosing which workshop topics to address and how often to repeat particular workshops. In addition to planning and conducting phase groups and skill-building workshops, rehab practitioners met individual consumers at least monthly for one hour to complete monthly summaries of their progress. They were required to document how the workshops were moving consumers toward their goals and to summarize their monthly visits with individual consumers.

The IPRT Team

IPRT teams included professionals with undergraduate or graduate degrees in a variety of helping professions. Kolap's team was no exception.

The supervisor, Cindy Whitaker, had an M.S.W and a license to practice therapy. She had been at the agency for 15 years and Kolap thought of her as both "motherly" and "detail oriented." A strong Catholic, Cindy valued addressing matters of spirituality with consumers.

Rehab practitioner Troy Kurosky had a B.A. in Psychology and started working in the IPRT Program the same week as Kolap. Kolap viewed him as "smart and intellectual, but self-conscious" because he lacked a masters degree. Kolap thought he conducted "good workshops" and had "good perspectives." Though his grandparents were from Poland, he was a very "westernized American." Previously Catholic, he described Catholicism as "too rigid and too structured," the reason for his always "feeling guilty." As an adult, he had adopted Buddhist beliefs.

Linda Schram had a B.A. in Psychology and also started working in the IPRT Program the same week as Kolap. Kolap thought of her as "the creative one in the group," doing workshops on such things as "creative healing." She was of Italian background and a self-described "Pagan."

Deborah Brown, an African-American, had a B.S. in speech and on-the-job training in Continuing Day Treatment. She had been at the agency for more than 20 years, but had frequently moved among positions when agency restructuring had dictated that a social work degree or license was required to fulfill particular positions. As the only part-time rehab practitioner, she had been in the IPRT Program for 8 years. If program policies changed, she would lose her current position to someone with more relevant degrees. As a result, she could end up with a new position that paid less and was less challenging. Kolap thought that Deborah was sometimes "confrontational, strong-willed, and opinionated." She identified herself as a Christian.

Despite their significant professional and spiritual diversity, the team was very collegial. In fact, Kolap considered it one of the most cohesive IPRT teams. Even though she had limited experience, colleagues viewed her as an informal leader on the team and consulted her regarding curriculum development, training, and grants.

Kolap Chonn White

Kolap Chonn grew up with hair-raising stories of her family's suffering as the Vietnam War spilled over into Cambodia. The Khmer Rouge overtook most of Cambodia in the 1970s, except for Rheem, the city where Kolap was born. The nearby naval base provided an easy escape from Rheem because Kolap's father was a captain in the Khmer Navy. Sneaking aboard her father's ship one night, the Khmer Rouge offered those aboard "peaceful surrender," promising that they could return to their homes safely. Kolap's father, suspicious of this offer, prohibited his family from leaving the ship. Relief filled the family when they later discovered that all those who left the ship had been executed and that their own house had been looted and burned. They had no choice but to leave Cambodia for the U.S., one of the very few countries accepting political refugees at the time.

The fourth of five children, Kolap was just 20 days old when her family arrived in the U.S. The government had relocated their relatives to various parts of the U.S., but Kolap's family settled in a small coal-mining town in Pennsylvania. Several years later they relocated again, this time to a Pennsylvania Dutch community. The only Asian family in a nearly all-white community, they re-created and preserved Khmer culture inside their own home and Kolap became aware of the differences between herself and those in her community. For Kolap's family, the contrast between Khmer living and western culture was as drastic as night and day.

As a child, Kolap knew that she was different. During the Vietnam era, some Americans came to hate anyone who looked Asian—like Kolap's family. She noticed when people whispered, looked at her, and moved out of the way to avoid contact. Almost everywhere she went she got angry stares and heard comments that she could not understand because, at the time, she only spoke Khmer. Khmer culture also had distinct gender roles—something else that made her different. Girls were not to leave the house for any reason, yet boys could do what they wanted. Khmer girls stayed home while "western" girls went out.

Many of the families in Kolap's rural Pennsylvania community were nominally Christian, not Buddhist like her family. She viewed her Christian classmates' "partying" on the weekend as hypocritical and became very "anti-Christian" in high school.

After high school, Kolap attended the University of New York at Buffalo on a scholarship, majoring in public health. It was difficult for her to leave her tight-knit Asian family, but it was there that she became a Christian after a Youth for Christ leader befriended her. His demonstration of Christian love contrasted sharply with what she had experienced in high school.

When she became a Christian, Kolap's parents worried that she had become part of a cult. As traditional Khmer, they believed in Buddhism and its related animism. In America, however, they "worshipped the god of success" and pushed their children to be doctors or otherwise successful in their careers. Kolap did not hold this same view, but believed that living a successful life meant pleasing and serving Christ. So, after completing her undergraduate program in three years, Kolap immediately enrolled in a Master of Social Work Program offering a track in clinical social work.

After completing her first year of the two-year MSW Program, Kolap began considering work as a missionary. With a friend's encouragement, Kolap prayed, read God's Word, and became certain that God was calling her to Cambodia as a missionary and public health worker.

Though excited that she wanted to visit her heritage and homeland, Kolap's parents were also frightened about her going to Cambodia. They were proud that Kolap wanted to discover her roots, but confused as to why she would go as a servant of Christ rather than as a tourist. They also had misgivings about her going to Steng Treng, a province in Cambodia with high rates of poverty, malaria, and AIDS.

Kolap went to the mission field unsure of how God would use her. But in Cambodia she came to believe that God was more interested in working *in* a person than *through* a person. Her time there sometimes felt like a "trial by fire." As Kolap explained, "When God tested my faithfulness to him, my perseverance, and my issues with pride, identity, and forgiveness, I gained a deeper understanding of His love for me." Kolap came to understand that God viewed her as "unclean" but loved her anyway, just as she loved the Khmer children who were covered with scabies and smelled of urine. And Kolap concluded, "His goal for me in Cambodia was simply that I experience who I really am: a sinner with no one to run to but Him."

Returning home after a year in Cambodia, Kolap completed her MSW in June 2000, got married in August, and moved across the state to Albany where she began working in the IPRT Program in October. As a Rehabilitation Practitioner II, Kolap enjoyed creating workshops in which consumers could explore spiritual issues in addition to more conventional mental health topics. Many consumers in Kolap's workshops had deep-seated anger, mistrust, and grief issues about sexual abuse, physical abuse, alcohol abuse, and interpersonal relationships. She thought this was a great opportunity to discuss difficult topics such as free will, agape love, justice, mercy, pain, and suffering. However, she worked hard to conduct these kinds of workshops in a way that was respectful of diverse views about spirituality and did not impose her values or views on the consumers.

Kolap and her husband joined a small nondenominational church with roots in the Plymouth Brethren movement. Kolap enjoyed the Christ-centered teaching of the church, but at times struggled with how to reconcile her views with those in her church that could sometimes be rather "legalistic" and "old school conservative," particularly on issues such as the submission and role of women.

Many people at her church didn't understand what social workers do—a few even viewed the psychotherapy aspect of social work as "evil." In fact, Kolap's own husband sometimes questioned the validity of helping professions like social work and psychology, wondering whether they were, as he said, "a human attempt to do God's work." Kolap found, though, that when she shared her views with others, people usually understood and respected them. She felt confident, "If I'm where God wants me to be, then His Spirit will work through me and He will send people to me for help." As a result, Kolap didn't get angry or upset when others misunderstood what she did as a social worker.

Her personal worldview supported her attempts to enable her consumers to consider their own worldviews—consumers like Cathy who had attended several of Kolap's workshops.

Cathy Crider

Cathy Crider was a large, African-American woman who enrolled in IPRT in January 2001, just three months after Kolap began at the agency. She first met Kolap when she joined her Phase I group. Initially, Kolap noted that Cathy was unkempt, often not bathing and wearing baggy clothes with her hair tucked under a hat. Nevertheless, Kolap recognized that Cathy had very proper manners and was polite, dignified, and articulate—rather unusual traits compared to other consumers in the IPRT Program.

As she worked in the Phase I group to clarify the values that impacted important areas of her life, Cathy talked about the goals of family and work. She wanted to get married and have children, but none of her boyfriends "ever worked out." She also talked of her experience moving from the deep South, where she was raised, to upstate New York, where she lived and worked all her adult life. Work was important to her, and at one time she had been promoted to a business management position. However, what should have been feelings of accomplishment resulted in feelings of conflict when Cathy became the boss to friends who thought she had become a "white girl."

From Cathy's case file, Kolap knew that Cathy had last worked in January 1999, more than two years before she enrolled in IPRT. Cathy reportedly stopped working because of her life-long depression, but when her short-term medical disability ended, she was referred to IPRT. Though she had a primary care physician, Cathy did not see him because she had no insurance. Initially self-pay at IPRT, Cathy eventually received Medicaid and disability, though she viewed it as dehumanizing and embarrassing.

About six months after enrolling in IPRT, Cathy also joined Kolap's workshop on Forgiveness. Because of her work with Cathy in the Phase I group, Kolap knew that Cathy was bright, insightful, and self-aware, and quickly realized that she was also familiar with the Bible. She understood the concept of forgiveness but acknowledged struggling to give and receive it. Cathy discussed growing up in the church and being very involved with it up until a couple of years before coming to IPRT. Kolap sensed that, though Cathy seemed to have some belief in God, she was dealing with a lot of pain because of her family history.

"Are you angry at God?" Kolap once questioned.

"No," Cathy replied matter-of-factly. "I've always been taught not to be angry at or question God."

Cathy went on to talk about how she still attended a church sporadically, but was not committed to it. Kolap suspected that Cathy stopped going to God for understanding and help because she was really mad at God, though afraid to admit that.

When Cathy told Kolap about feeling marginalized by church and family, Kolap could sympathize. She knew what it was liked to feel marginalized from the mainstream, though not for the same reasons as Cathy. Many of the challenging experiences that Kolap had growing up were related to "cliques," and she was often the one on the outside looking in. Kolap also sensed that Cathy really trusted her because they could relate to each other and because she seemed to understand what Cathy was experiencing.

Faith in Practice

Consistent with the IRPT model, Kolap did not view her workshops as therapy per se. Nevertheless, skill-building workshops often evoked issues that consumers could then discuss with their therapists. Kolap had volunteered to conduct a variety of workshops on communication skills, mental health and wellness, anger management, social skills, as well as the education and vocational workshops. One workshop Kolap never volunteered to teach was the Self-esteem and Confidence workshop. Because she didn't believe self-esteem came from within, she didn't want to teach something with which she disagreed. Fortunately, she was never asked to teach it.

Kolap proposed the Mental Health and Spirituality workshop because of how often consumers seemed to raise spiritual issues in their discussions with her. Based on Kolap's work record and her own beliefs, Cindy Whitaker readily supported the proposed workshop. Nevertheless, Kolap felt some anxiety about explicitly addressing spiritual issues in a public setting. Her anxiety diminished after several weeks because clients seemed to respond so well. The discussions were unusually engaging and personal.

Cathy enrolled in several of Kolap's workshops before taking her Mental Health and Spirituality workshop. As a result, Kolap knew a great deal about the influences in Cathy's childhood. Cathy had discussed the influence of growing up in Alabama where church was a "fashion show," women wore a different dress every week, and the church taught that people were naturally good. Cathy had learned that they weren't and had discussed the church's power and influence in her family, where her father had a lot of control. Cathy viewed both her church in the south and her church in the north as "very African-American" and "charismatic," but viewed herself as "very white."

The Mental Health and Spirituality workshop required that participants use an interpretive lens to think about their faith. It was in this workshop that Kolap noted how Cathy's image of God was blurred, like it was for many people, with the image of her own father. In the workshop discussions, Cathy eventually disclosed that she hated her father because he had been violent and abusive. Cathy also expressed anger towards her mother for knowing about the abuse but not doing anything to stop it. As a result of these comments, Kolap began to understand why Cathy viewed men as dominating and hated women who were too submissive.

Kolap observed in the workshop that Cathy was a woman who really absorbed what she was reading and learning and actively engaged in the group discussions. It also seemed that Cathy had trouble handling all the emotions the workshops provoked.

One day after a workshop, troubled and struggling, Cathy asked Kolap, "What was your mom like?"

"Very Asian and submissive," Kolap disclosed. "All she has ever known was the Asian culture's view of women."

The conversation with Cathy reaffirmed the conclusion Kolap had come to some time ago—that being a non-traditional Asian woman with a traditional Asian mother was not hard for her as an adult. Somehow, she had learned to hold onto the positive aspects of her mother's Khmer traditions and let go of things that were not. She knew who she was in Christ and she wasn't ashamed of her Khmer heritage or the intense struggles and persecution that she and her family experienced. She also knew that these things made her a good rehab practitioner because she could understand different kinds of people from different kinds of backgrounds. She, herself, knew what it was like to grow up in a western society with very Asian parents.

"Isn't that hard for you—as an Asian woman?" Cathy wondered aloud. "Do you want to be like her?"

From prior workshop discussions, Kolap knew Cathy understood that traditional Asian women were typically submissive and passive. Nevertheless, Cathy's curiosity about the role of women, and the personal question, startled Kolap.

Why would she ask me this? I didn't know she was so interested in my mother. She seems to be relying on me too much. I haven't even thought this through yet.

Almost immediately, Kolap felt a tinge of self-conscious uncertainty. *How much of myself do I disclose? For me, faith has made all the difference. How can I respond without mentioning that? Should I?*

Later, in another session, Cathy struggled to write about her own mother's role in the family. Kolap prompted her to begin by thinking about herself and how she was different from her parents. Cathy wrote pages and pages. After Kolap asked whether Cathy saw any difference between the way she viewed her mother and how she presented herself, Cathy was able to discuss with the group her own issues with "Southern black women," how her mother fit this stereotype, and how she didn't view herself like this. She felt different because she was college educated, did not speak with a southern accent, and was considered a "free thinker" who would not easily sway to a man's opinion—or anyone else's for that matter.

Is she projecting her own views of what her mother was like? Is she wondering how or how not to fit into the mold of her own mother? Kolap wondered. She suspected that Cathy thought traditional roles for women might be hard for Kolap because these were hard for Cathy herself. Kolap thought that Cathy, in some ways, identified with her because their mothers filled very traditional roles while they themselves did not.

"What was it like," Cathy asked after one session, "growing up knowing you were so different from your mother?"

"It was very difficult," Kolap acknowledged. "I went through many identity crises trying to understand who I was in this western world—where I considered people to be rude and obnoxious. I became very skillful in being able to read other people and understanding myself in relation to them."

Kolap continued, describing to Cathy the barriers of language, color, and the Vietnam War, and the apparent resentment that people felt about her coming to "their country."

Most importantly, Kolap described how she "learned to count on God for support, not man."

Later, Kolap wondered, *Was that disclosure appropriate for a professional social worker, especially in a public agency?* She wasn't sure. But Cathy seemed interested and grateful.

Several weeks later, Cathy came late to Kolap's Spirituality and Mental Health workshop appearing troubled and unsettled. Kolap did not try to engage her during the session, not wanting to "open a can of worms" when there was not much time in the group to discuss her issues. After group, as others left, Cathy sat quietly while Kolap cleaned up the group room.

Tentatively, Kolap approached her. "Are you OK? You seem upset today."

"Kolap," Cathy exclaimed quietly, "I don't mean to be rude, but I hate this workshop!"

"Why," Kolap asked deliberately, "do you feel that way?" Even while she listened for an answer, her mind raced ahead, *Am I interfering with Cathy's life? Violating a boundary?*

It's hard to think about it for two hours," Cathy replied, "and then leave it behind."

Kolap's anxiety soared. She had wondered how consumers would respond to the material in this workshop, especially because the agency did not encourage content related to Christianity. But out loud, she asked, "Maybe you should just take a break from the group for a while?"

"Maybe?" Cathy asked.

And then, aware that she was probably doing too much rescuing, Kolap added, "I understand if it's too hard."

In the car on the way home, Kolap teared up. *I feel like a failure. Maybe I should revamp the workshop. Maybe this isn't God's will.* Suddenly overwhelmed with her own feelings of inadequacy, Kolap asked herself, *Who do I think I am, running this group?*

10

I'm Not the Church Social Worker!

Mary Anne Poe

"What should I do, Sue?" church member Carla Rushing pleaded. "Gloria just called and said, 'We've solved the car problem for you.' The church found a used Taurus for $4,500. She told me to come to the church right away to sign the loan. They want me to work in the nursery on Sunday and Wednesday nights to help pay for it and since it's Christmas break, they said Mark can work at the church, too, to help pay for it. They said it would be good for him to see that he needs to be responsible and help me.'"

"Slow down a bit, Carla," Sue Stanford said trying to remain calm in the face of Carla's apparent panic.

"I don't know what to do," Carla continued, collapsing into sobs. "I don't want to sign a loan. I can't afford that. I can't make my son work over his Christmas break to pay for my car."

Broyton Community Church

Broyton Community Church (BCC) was a conservative, evangelical congregation, not affiliated with a particular denomination. The church had about 1500 members and held traditional views on women's roles and on marriage and divorce. The church had all the ministries found in large congregations—Sunday School, discipleship groups, youth program, preschool, musical groups for all

Development of this decision case was supported in part by the University of South Carolina College of Social Work. It was prepared solely to provide material for class discussion and not to suggest either effective or ineffective handling of the situation depicted. While based on field research regarding an actual situation, names and certain facts may have been disguised to protect confidentiality. The author and editors wish to thank the anonymous case reporter for cooperation in making this account available for the benefit of social work students and practitioners.

ages, fellowship suppers, women's ministries, and in recent years had begun to emphasize men's programs such as men's accountability groups.

Steve Parker, the pastor of the church, was a strong and decisive leader who had been at the church for about twenty years. He was loved and respected in the congregation. Steve did very little personal counseling, usually making referrals to a few select Christian counselors. He explained to Sue that the pastor should not get too involved in the details of his parishioners' lives so that he could "be their pastor." Sue was not particularly impressed with this pastoral philosophy, but Steve usually delivered what she felt was a good sermon. Sue thought that Steve probably worked to "save the marriage at all costs" when helping people such as Carla.

Lay involvement in care ministries was encouraged and usually organized through small discipleship groups and Sunday School classes led by lay members. Marsha Baker and Gloria Gibbs, were two key leaders of women's discipleship groups. They were strong leaders, vocal believers in prayer and submission to God's will, but lacked any formal education about many of the issues facing the women in their classes. They felt called by God to help hurting women and had begun a study group on Wednesday nights called Healing Our Hurts. About twenty women attended the class.

Sue Stanford

Sue Stanford had been a church social worker for ten years in two other cities before moving to Broyton. She had a BSW and MSW degree from the University of North Carolina and had completed a master's degree in theology at Duke Divinity School. Her work in the churches included providing a full range of services to members and to the community. In this capacity she counseled numerous women in abusive relationships and supported them in the various stages of staying and leaving. She always maintained good working relationships with services in the community for victims of domestic violence and worked diligently to help other pastoral staff members understand the dynamics of such relationships. Of course, as a church social worker, she helped individuals and families with all kinds of problems and knew that positive relationships with other professionals in the community were vital.

Sue and her family moved to Broyton in 1995 because of a job opportunity for her husband. No church social work jobs were available, so Sue began working in an agency providing behavioral health services. She was the director of community educational programs. She enjoyed having a chance to be a layperson without professional responsibilities in her worship context. Through her new job she networked with service providers in most of the local social service agencies. She served on several task forces and boards, including a local faith-based program providing a full range of services for families with low-income, a drug abuse prevention coalition, the advisory council for the local university's social work department, and the state's domestic violence coalition.

Carla Rushing's Troubles

Carla Rushing had already experienced one failed marriage and had two teenage sons, Mark and Andy, before she began dating Rob seven years previously. Rob had also been married and divorced. Both had been members of BCC for many years. When Carla became pregnant, Rob wanted her to get an abortion but she refused to do this. Instead, they were counseled by the pastor and others in the church to marry. This is what they did. Rob moved into the house that Carla had owned since her divorce eight years earlier. Ben was born soon after they married and Jon followed two years later. Carla now had four sons.

Troubles in the marriage were evident from the beginning. Rob had a drug and alcohol problem. Early in their relationship, Carla had "experimented" with drugs on a couple of occasions. She never became addicted or even involved beyond the two or three times they went to parties together. Carla worked full-time as a client aide at a sheltered workshop for those with developmental disabilities while Rob's work was sporadic. He helped on construction projects and Carla never knew the terms of his employment. The crisis came when Rob was arrested on a drug charge. In the process of legal proceedings, Carla's house of cards collapsed. She discovered that Rob had spent all her savings, mortgaged their home, and apparently accumulated thousands of dollars in debt. As Rob faced the consequences of his criminal charge and the reality of his drug problem, it appeared that he would finally get the treatment he needed for his addictions. But the financial picture was too bleak. They would have to file bankruptcy and move from their home.

The Church Helps

At that point, the church became very involved. Carla shared her problems with the discipleship group led by Gloria and Marsha, and they shifted into high gear to solve her problems. In conversation with the pastor, Marsha arranged counseling for Carla and Rob with a Christian counselor contracted by the church to supplement the work of the pastor. Gloria had a son who had successfully completed an intensive residential Christian drug treatment program and she encouraged Rob and Carla to give it a chance. Rob agreed to participate in this program if the church could arrange his admission. The church also agreed to help pay for this treatment. Rob was soon out of the home and participating in the treatment program. Carla agreed to be supportive of her husband in his efforts to overcome addiction.

The pastor organized a committee of lay helpers to oversee the use of money given on Carla and Rob's behalf. The committee included Marsha, Gloria and several deacons. Marsha and Gloria were assigned to Carla, while two men were assigned to Rob for accountability purposes. Carla's expenses were mounting because Rob supplied no income to the family now.

Carla emphasized to Marsha and Gloria, "I want the marriage to work, but if Rob does not complete this treatment program, I am finished with him!"

Marsha replied, "Gloria's son did so well in this program, I am sure this will help Rob. Just trust the Lord in this."

"I can't live with this any more. He scares me with his drug use. I never know what is going to happen. I think he is influencing my older boys, too," Carla reported to her church helpers. "I am afraid that they are drinking and using now, too."

Several church groups, including Carla and Rob's Sunday school class, collected sizable offerings for the family, literally thousands of dollars over a period of three months. Gloria found a house for Carla to rent and made arrangements for Carla and her children to move. Gloria and Marsha worked up a "contract" for Carla in which they agreed for the church to pay her rent for at least the next six months while Rob was in treatment. They would monitor her finances and she would have to be accountable to them. The financial problems were big, though. Her job at a local sheltered workshop did not provide enough income to meet her monthly needs for shelter, food, automobile, and childcare. She needed ongoing financial support. In December, the class wanted her to have plenty of cash so that she could shop for Christmas presents for her children and they donated generously. A year later, the class discovered that Marsha had intercepted the donations and shopped for Carla's children, wrapped the packages, and put them under Carla's tree.

Since Rob could not leave the treatment program, Carla made the three hour trip to the treatment center almost every Sunday afternoon so the younger boys, now ages two and four, could see their daddy. Carla's older boys visited occasionally because Rob had been their "daddy" for the past four years. After two months in the program, Rob was allowed to come home occasionally. On one occasion, he helped the family move from their home into the rental house that Marsha and Gloria had found for the family.

Sue Gets Involved

As a church member, Sue had been a rather uninvolved observer in the Sunday School class until she helped with the move to the rental house. She made several monetary donations and had been the one to suggest that Christmas money be given directly to Carla so that she could select the gifts for her children. She knew very few details about Carla's life, just that the class had been praying for them and that Rob was away in a treatment program. Their first real conversation occurred the day that Carla moved. The whole class helped with the move, but for about an hour during the day, Sue and Carla stayed together at her "old" home to finish some packing. The contrast between the nice house that the bank had reclaimed and the new rental house that was about to be Carla's home with two little boys was extreme. This was when Sue began to realize the extent of Carla's distress, her risk in relation to Rob, and the lay helpers' lack of awareness about the dynamics of abusive relationships. Carla described to Sue an emotionally cruel and controlling relationship with Rob, "Rob likes to have things his way. He doesn't think I do anything right. He says things I wish the boys didn't hear."

"Like what kind of things?" Sue asked.

"Oh, I'm sure he doesn't mean it. He says he thinks I am stupid, calls me a bitch. I don't like for the boys to see him when he's like that. Frankly, it's been easier since he's been in the treatment program."

"Sounds like he is a bit of a bully," Sue replied.

"He just thinks he doesn't have to do any of the work around here. He plays with the boys some, but it is usually too rough for me. "

Carla also described the attempts to "save the marriage" in the marriage counseling arranged by Marsha. It was obvious that Carla felt indebted to the church for all the help and repeated over and over again how much had been done and how guilty she felt for needing such help.

"I'm so embarrassed that this house is such a mess," Carla said repeatedly as Sue helped her sort through toys and clothes in the boys' room. "I just can't seem to get organized."

"Moving is always a mess," Sue assured her.

At lunch, when all those helping with the move were gathered, Gloria declared, "I am so thankful for all the help this class has been to Carla. It is fortunate that we were able to find this place for her to live."

Sue cringed inside, seeing the embarrassment on Carla's face and newly aware of how Gloria and Marsha exerted control in Carla's life through helping.

Rob Quits Treatment

Marsha and Gloria kept constant vigilance on Carla's condition and needs. One of them called daily to ask how she was and to learn what she was doing. When Rob was dismissed from the program for failure to comply with the rules, they told her that he could not move back into her house. Carla followed their instructions and told him he could not move back with her. Someone at the treatment center told Carla that Rob had a "problem with authority." Rob moved back to Broyton, initially staying with his mother. He eventually got his own apartment and became more involved at church. He grew particularly close to one other man, Chuck Sawyer, his accountability partner.

Carla was still reluctant to file for divorce, though she had managed the household while Rob was away and had grown to enjoy the relative peace of his absence. She had grown more independent and had begun to realize how terrible their relationship had been. Carla began to wonder if it could possibly be okay with God if she divorced. Now that Rob was back in town, she dreaded contact with him because he continually harassed her about moving back into the house and about visiting with the little boys. Rob's mother also hassled and irritated her.

Carla Files for Divorce

One Sunday morning, after Rob had been back in Broyton for about three weeks, Sue asked Carla how things were going. Carla confided that Rob had failed a drug screen—one of the regular screens mandated by the court due to his criminal record.

"I think it may be time to get a divorce," Carla said to Sue. "I'm afraid for my boys." She then collapsed into tears. After Sue found a quiet place in the church building where they could talk, Carla went on, "I've not said this to anyone else. Rob is getting the papers for divorce this Friday. I don't want everyone to know my business."

As Sue and Carla talked, the depth of the problem with the church helpers grew more and more clear to Sue.

"Marsha and Gloria talk with my counselor, others in my discipleship group, Brother Steve, and Rob's friends. Everyone knows all my business."

Carla also explained that she was afraid of Rob and what he would do when served the divorce papers.

"Have you had any contact with The Women's Place?" Sue asked. The Women's Place was the local agency serving the needs of those experiencing domestic violence, and Sue knew the staff at the agency well.

"Another friend suggested that to me but Marsha warned me not to work with them. They are not a Christian agency," Carla responded.

"Please call The Women's Place, Carla. They can help you," Sue encouraged. She told Carla what she knew about the agency and that, while the agency was not "Christian," several of the staff members were, in fact, believers.

Sue was also concerned for Carla's safety and explained the importance of having a "safety plan." As they talked, Sue felt she had to be more involved at this point. *I know I don't have a professional role in this situation,* she thought, *But if I don't get involved, that seems both professionally and spiritually irresponsible; Carla is really at risk here.*

The next day, Monday, Carla phoned Sue, "I called The Women's Place this morning."

"What happened?" Sue asked.

"I told them about Rob getting the divorce papers on Friday. They wanted to know if I felt safe and then they started helping me think about how to handle things."

"I'm glad you called them, Carla. You sound relieved. I think they can help you."

"They suggested I get an order of protection. They said they could help me do that. I have to work on Friday. I'm afraid I'm about to lose my job because of all this, Sue."

"Why would you lose your job, Carla?" Sue asked.

"Just all the calls. Rob calls, Gloria calls, I have to call my lawyers. The day care calls. And I'm afraid that Rob will go get the boys after he gets the papers," Carla began to cry.

"Is there a way I can help next Friday, Carla?" Sue asked as she realized the depth of Carla's despair.

"I don't know, Sue. I don't want to bother you."

"Carla, this is a good time for you to have plenty of help. I want you and the boys to be safe."

Carla, with Sue's help and the help of The Women's Place, arranged to get her younger boys from day care early, so that Rob would not be able to get them. Carla planned to stay at the shelter until she felt safe to return home.

"What about your older boys, Carla? What will they do?" Sue knew that they would not be allowed at the shelter with Carla and the little boys.

"Mark is mad at me. He's all tied up in this, too. When I told him about my plan for the shelter, he got all tough. I told him to go to his dad's house."

"What did he say?" Sue asked.

"He said he wouldn't leave the house-that it was his home. He could take care of Rob. Sue, he can't take care of Rob. They will get into it. I've seen them get into it before. I wanted him to go stay with his dad. He's never been very close to Rob. Rob always favored Andy and picked on Mark."

"What about Andy?" asked Sue.

"He's in Colorado, thank goodness. I haven't even talked to him yet. No telling what he will do. Mark's home for the summer, but he doesn't have his driver's license. I'm afraid for Mark."

"Did the Women's Place have any suggestions for you about Mark?" asked Sue.

"They just said he couldn't stay in the shelter and that he would have to make up his own mind. They said they would talk with him if he wanted," said Carla.

"Will he talk with them?" Sue responded.

"I don't think so. He's trying to be tough and thinks I am crazy," Carla said.

"Well, he's an adult, Carla. You can't make him do anything. He has to make his own choices at this point," Sue replied, feeling somewhat desperate herself for Carla's situation and all the complexity and danger of it. She hoped that at least Carla would follow through on the plan that she had developed with the shelter and for her little boys.

Trying to Get Untangled

Carla did go to the shelter on Friday and returned home after about a week. In the parenting plan, court ordered in the divorce proceedings, Carla had requested that Rob's visitation with the boys be supervised because of his drug problem. He had tested positive on several occasions since leaving treatment. Rob had taken the boys from her home when Carla thought he was high but she had been unable to stop him. The court ordered visitation for every other weekend. His mother was to supervise. He was subject to drug tests whenever requested by Carla or her attorney.

Rob continued to come to church. He boasted to others in the church of his love for Carla and the boys and his desire to be reunited. He maintained a close relationship with his "accountability partner," a man he had known all his life and had even lived next door to for many years. Rob always came to church and made a point of seeing his boys. He would take them from Sunday school to play on the church's playground while Carla was in Sunday school. When she would arrive to pick up the boys, he would use the opportunity to harass and belittle her, often accusing her in front of the boys of trying to keep them away from him. Though there was a "no contact" order of protection, he was ignoring it while on the church grounds.

One Sunday, Rob was particularly threatening. On this occasion, Carla asked the boys' teacher and the Minister to Children to help her get to her car safely. Because Rob was generally careful to say things to Carla when others could not actually witness it, Carla's attorney subsequently filed a contempt of court motion and subpoenaed the Children's Minister and teacher.

Carla was grasping for some emotional support from her church helpers and the staff. She continued to feel so guilty about all her needs and embarrassed that so many people were getting dragged into her dirty business. Carla and Sue talked several times a week. Carla often seemed confused about what to do. Sue wanted to stay connected with her because of the extreme emotional distress that Carla exhibited.

"Marsha called," Carla reported one day. "She makes me feel so bad when she calls, like she's in charge of everything I do."

"What does she say?" Sue asked.

"She wants all my receipts so she knows what I have spent. She nags me about paying bills. I don't know. It's just the way she says things more than anything. I feel so judged. She wants to run Mark's life, too. She tells me what to make him do as though he's five years old. I can't make my grown son do anything."

"Sounds like you are not feeling much support from Marsha," Sue reflected back to Carla.

"I don't. They are supposed to be helping me, but I can hardly think, they are so demanding," Carla blubbered. "Sometimes I think I'm going crazy, but they got this house for me and pay the rent."

Sue became concerned about Carla's apparent depression. "Are you still seeing the counselor at The Women's Place?" Sue asked.

"Yes, she wants me to see my doctor about getting some medicine for depression, but Marsha tells me I don't need medicine. I just need to trust the Lord. I've made my bed, now I have to lie in it, is what Marsha thinks."

"Maybe you should just quit talking to Marsha so much," said Sue.

"That's what the counselor says to me," Carla replied.

As time went on, Carla seemed to depend more and more on Sue's encouragement and the help of the therapist at The Women's Place that Carla now saw once a week. Sue thought that Carla's spiritual and emotional pain was growing because of the very controlling approach that Marsha and Gloria had assumed in their relationship with her. Carla now felt as much pressure from them as she had once felt from Rob, came to feel that she was inadequate and unworthy, and thought that she should follow their directives. Now, she had to handle their onslaught of well-meaning, but harmful, "help" as well as try to wrest herself free from Rob's manipulation and control.

In Court

Though she had known him for years, Carla had had no direct contact with Steve, her pastor, during this whole process until they saw each other in court. She was accompanied by her attorney while Rob appeared with his attorney, his accountability partner, and Sue and Rob's son, Andy. Carla's attorney asked the Sunday school teacher and Children's Minister to testify on her behalf. The pastor came to court with these two staff members, but Carla felt the clear message was that the church was not taking any sides in their battle. He hardly spoke to her and seemed to be there for Rob as much as for her. The very fact of their involvement in it embarrassed Carla, but their unwillingness to support her hurt deeply. She did not think she had done anything that made her responsible for the trouble now. Rob's attorney got Andy, their son, to testify on Rob's behalf. Carla was devastated that her own son had testified against her and that he had even lied on the witness stand about what Rob had done at church. She hated the way that Rob was using her own son against her and devastated that Andy would comply.

Carla decided to ask for a meeting with the pastor soon after they had been in court. Carla knew that Pastor Steve was aware of many of the details of her life from Marsha's and Gloria's perspective because they often reported to her what he had said she should do. When Carla asked for her support, Sue agreed to accompany her. This meeting was prompted partly by Carla's experience in court in which she felt no support from the church. The meeting with Pastor Steve did not go well. He listened to Carla's side of the story, but offered no real compassion or empathy to her. Instead, he asserted again his need not to get in the middle of their domestic quarrels and that the church could not abandon either Rob or her. Carla longed for Pastor Steve's approval to divorce Rob and move on, but it was not forthcoming.

The Final Straw

In spite of all the turmoil, Carla was slowly gaining a sense of self and feeling stronger. She still had major financial worries because her full-time job left her still $200 short each month. Rob was not providing child support as ordered by the court. Every week was filled with various forms of harassment from him. Marsha and Gloria continued to call. Each call left her feeling judged and inadequate. Carla was participating in a support group for survivors of domestic violence and seeing a therapist once a week. Legal proceedings seemed to drag on and attorney fees were mounting, but Carla was beginning to see the light at the end of the tunnel. She battled depression constantly, having some good days and some very low ones. She had developed a workable schedule for her little boys. Usually the only tough days with them were after they returned from visits with their dad. Carla continued to attend church regularly and even seemed to be gaining spiritual strength as she felt God caring for her and providing for her needs. Through their conversations, Sue knew that Carla was still on a bit of a roller coaster ride, but managing.

Then, one day, Carla called. "My car has broken down," she began anxiously. "I've got to get it towed. What am I going to do about work? I can't pay for car repair bills?" Carla grew more and more agitated as she talked about this new financial crisis.

Sue tried to slow her down. "Okay, let's think through the possibilities, Carla."

"I've already had a friend look at it," moaned Carla. "He said it's a major job. The car's hardly worth the cost to repair it."

Can anyone help for the next few days while you work out a solution?" Sue asked.

"My son is here and can help for a few days, but he has school and a job, too. Can you just pray for me that something will work out?"

"Sure, you know I will do that." Sue responded.

"I've got to go. I'm at work and someone's paging me." Carla said.

The next day Sue discussed with her husband the possibility of loaning Carla a third car they had but did not really need at this time. They were holding onto it for their fifteen-year-old child who would be driving soon. She called Carla to tell her that she could use this car for several months. Carla had just talked with Gloria. She had just called to tell Carla that the pastor had bought a car through the church for her, a 2000 Taurus, for $4500. He had called a church member who owned a car dealership to explain the need. Gloria told Carla that she needed to come to the church to sign the loan. The church expected her to pay $75 a month and to begin to work at the church providing child care on Sunday and Wednesday nights to help pay for it. Since Carla's son was home for the Christmas holidays, Gloria said that the church would put him to work in order to help pay for it as well. Gloria said this would help him understand Carla's need for help and make him responsible. Carla was overwhelmed. She could not afford $75 a month. She did not want another job. And she did not appreciate that they had an expectation for her college-age son to work for her car. He already had a job and school.

Carla had not asked for this "help." Gloria had called the day before and Carla had mentioned the car problems, but only with the request for her prayers, just like she had asked Sue. How could they think this had solved her problem? For Carla, this effort by the church felt like an impossible burden—more indebtedness for her financially as well as emotionally, theft of her responsibility to solve her own problems, and more judgment from her church family.

Sue's Dilemma

Sue could hear the desperation in Carla's voice. Fearing that Carla's growing independence was about to collapse, she also wondered, *Is Carla about to have an emotional break? Is this spiritual abuse?* Sue felt increasingly troubled and angry. *These people in my church are so insensitive toward Sue's condition. Even the pastor does not seem to understand,* she thought. *Is my own anger interfering with helping Carla? Can I continue to be a sort of bystander—talking with Carla when she calls and offering support to her but not intervening in any way with my church? Have I become a part of that abuse by not being willing to get involved with the church helpers or staff to advocate for Carla? I am not sure I could do any good anyway. I don't have much influence here. Maybe I should not interfere because no one at church has actually asked me to help? I can continue to talk with Carla when she calls. Is that enough? What should I do?*

11

THE THREAT

Mackenzi Huyser and Laura Zumdahl

It was a warm April morning as Scott Williams walked toward St. Andrews Medical Clinic. The neighborhood was strangely quiet given how warm the day was and how active the neighborhood usually became during the spring. As he got closer to the clinic he could see the staff shuffling around in the waiting area. As he reached the door, nurse Sarah Cox pointed, and yelled in a loud, frantic, "Here's Scott!" and raced toward the door to let him in.

St. Andrews Medical Clinic

Located on the north side of Chicago, St. Andrews Medical Clinic was a small clinic that provided health care to community residents who were homeless. The clinic was established as a free walk-in clinic where patients were served on a first-come, first-serve basis throughout the day. The clinic was open five days a week, with evening hours on Tuesday. Patients described the clinic as a "refuge" and many described the clinic as the "place that saved my life". The clinic was a warm place for patients, both physically and emotionally. The front waiting room was lined with large picture windows looking out to the street and tall plants filled the corners. Approximately 20 chairs were arranged back-to-back in the waiting room and a front desk lined the room opposite the windows. Two doors to the side of the front desk led to the back medical examination rooms and staff offices. Often the

Development of this decision case was supported in part by the University of South Carolina College of Social Work. It was prepared solely to provide material for class discussion and not to suggest either effective or ineffective handling of the situation depicted. While based on field research regarding an actual situation, names and certain facts may have been disguised to protect confidentiality. The author and editors wish to thank the anonymous case reporter for cooperation in making this account available for the benefit of social work students and practitioners.

waiting room was full of patients waiting to be seen.

The clinic was funded through a federal grant given to a local hospital. The purpose of the clinic was to serve the community and provide health care to a segment of the population that did not often receive health or prevention services, specifically in the clinic's community on the north side of Chicago. With no executive director or hospital administrator directly assigned to administer the clinic or provide on-site supervision, the clinic staff worked as a team to hold one another accountable and solved day-to-day issues that arose on their own.

Four full-time staff worked at the clinic and was considered the core team. These staff included Scott Williams, a BSW, Sarah Cox and Elizabeth Andrews, both registered nurses, and Robin Smith, the receptionist and office manager. The core team members held formal staff meetings every other week, but because of the nature of their work, they were often interacting on an hourly basis about the needs of patients. The other members of the team were all part-time or volunteers and included a half-time physician in addition to volunteer physicians. Specialists including a podiatrist, ophthalmologist, and physical therapist also provided voluntary services on a monthly basis. Legal services were available to patients two days a month and two part-time MSW social workers also were available for counseling services.

Scott Williams

Born and raised on the north side of Chicago, Scott Williams began volunteering in soup kitchens and homeless shelters when he was in high school. He developed a connection with those who were considered by others as "undesirables". To him, these "undesirables" were simply people looking for a connection and a way to fit in. He knew he could take the time to strike up a conversation with them or help them receive a warm meal.

In 1988 Scott graduated with a BSW from Trinity Christian College, a small Christian college located in a south suburb of Chicago. As a Christian Scott believed he could live out his faith by choosing social work as his vocation. Following graduation Scott moved back north and to the neighborhood where he grew up in Chicago. He interviewed for and was offered a position as case manager at St. Andrews Medical Clinic.

Scott enjoyed his work and saw it as an important part of the holistic services that the patients received while at the clinic. As the only full-time social worker and the employee who had been at St. Andrews the longest, Scott had the most consistent contact with the patients. He knew all of the patients by name and would often spend part of his day visiting with patients in the waiting room and also walking through the community to say "hello" and connect outside of the clinic. Scott also spent his time conducting intake assessments, making referrals to outside service providers, and dealing with crisis situations. He strongly believed that the clinic could help with short-term solutions and the problems would always continue; but as a social worker he also needed to advocate for having social services available in the community to help by addressing issues of housing, substance abuse, and basic needs such as food and clothing. Because of these ideas and the work he did in the community, Scott was seen by community leaders and social work educators as a great community resource, and frequently invited to speak at community events and in both undergraduate and graduate social work classes on the topics of homelessness and building community support systems. His fellow team members also looked to him for leadership, both in regards to serving clients' needs and managing the Clinic.

Fall 1999

In fall 1999, Jeff Richards came to the St. Andrews Medical Clinic to receive treatment for severe pain in his leg. Jeff was a tall, 50 year old, Caucasian male with a medium build. He presented no mental health history information at his intake, but through observation the clinic staff suspected he might be suffering with schizophrenia or another mental illness.

Jeff was diagnosed with peripheral neuropathy (nerve damage in the leg). Because Jeff had not tested positive for diabetes or other diseases related to peripheral neuropathy, the doctor believed it was more than likely caused from a previous injury and scheduled him for regular checkups to monitor him and prescribed prescription painkillers to be taken on a daily basis. Jeff was fairly consistent in showing up for his appointments, although he frequently complained to the staff that his visits to the clinic were keeping him from making the necessary arrangements to "move back to Belgium and save the orphanage." The visits also "slowed him down" and forced him to wait for medical treatment with the "lowest of the low."

"Royalty should not be treated like this," he often said aloud in the waiting room to no one in particular.

Although Jeff was fairly reliable with his appointments, he refused to take his medication with the same regularity. Scott had talked to Jeff about this, but often Jeff was aloof and didn't engage or express interest in this discussion with Scott. As a team, the staff discussed having Jeff come by the clinic each morning for his pills in an effort to help with this consistency. Jeff agreed to do this and for a while he was consistent in his attendance. Some days, however, when he was extremely delusional, he would verbally confront Sarah claiming loudly, "these pills are poisonous!" After a period of time when he wasn't showing up for his medication, Jeff cited his "high position in Belgian Royalty" as the reason for his absence. At one staff meeting Sarah expressed concerns about Jeff's mental health and her desire to see him undergo a mental health evaluation. She suggested, and the team agreed, if a window of opportunity would open, they might be able to have Jeff evaluated and medication for his mental illness could be prescribed.

Spring 2000

As Sarah unlocked the clinic door, Scott could see that she was shaking.

"What's going on?" he asked as he cautiously entered through the door and walked into the waiting area.

"Jeff was here not even five minutes ago; he was coming for his medication," Sarah explained. "I opened the door and when I started to hand him his medication, he didn't take it but looked at me with this strange look and came toward me with his arm cocked back. I thought he was going to hit me."

"What happened next?" Scott questioned.

"I yelled and slammed the door in his face," Sarah said loudly "and he took off running."

Scott looked around the waiting area; Elizabeth was standing by the front windows, and Robin was behind the front desk.

"Were all of you here when this happened?" Scott asked.

"Robin was here," Elizabeth responded, "but I was in the back office area when I heard Sarah yell."

"It was odd," Robin said quietly, "It was like any other day when he would show up for his medication, and all of a sudden he turned on Sarah."

"We need to get him evaluated," Elizabeth interrupted. "We have always talked about how we should get him to see someone for a mental health evaluation."

"That's true," Sarah agreed. "This was aggressive behavior and he should be evaluated."

"I don't know," Robin said cautiously. "True, it was odd behavior, but that's Jeff. That's how he acts. Plus, he's never physically threatened us before. This shouldn't be an excuse to have him evaluated."

"How do we know this isn't behavior we will continue to see?" Elizabeth questioned. "Do you want to open the door tomorrow and have the same thing happened to you?"

"Don't you think we could resolve this in a different way, other than just calling for a mental health evaluation?" Robin asked.

"Why don't you think a mental health evaluation will help him?" Sarah asked. "Perhaps it will help us better serve him."

"We know he suffers from some sort of mental illness," Elizabeth stated, "it isn't a bad thing to have him evaluated so we can give him the help he needs."

"That's true," Robin stated, "but what would this do to our relationship with Jeff? We know he trusts us. What would this involuntary evaluation do to that relationship?"

"Shouldn't we be concerned about his mental health and his treatment more than our relationship with him?" Elizabeth asked.

"If we don't maintain our relationship with him, who do we think will give him his medication or look out for his general well-being?" Robin asked.

"What do you think, Scott?" Elizabeth asked abruptly.

Scott thought, *It is clear that Sarah and Elizabeth want him to get evaluated Is this the best approach to dealing with the situation and helping Jeff in the long-run? Or are we doing him a disservice by not attending to his mental health? Is there any possible way to maintain our relationship with him and get him the help he needs?*

12

A Shoplifter?

George E. Huff, Michael E. Sherr, & Nelson Henning

"Good morning, Mrs. Clark," social worker Gary Cameron stood to greet a new client as she entered his office. "I am Mr. Cameron and I welcome you to the Mental Health Clinic (MHC). I was just . . ."

"I've been referred by the court," Mrs. Clark interrupted, "because I was arrested for shoplifting but I didn't mean to do it."

"I was just looking over the information that you filled out for the receptionist," Mr. Cameron started again. "She informed me that you told her that. Why don't you have a seat?"

"I meant it when I told her I didn't mean to do it," she continued, still standing. "I want you to understand that I don't remember doing it."

As the clinician on call, social worker Gary Cameron was accustomed to doing court-ordered assessments at a military mental health clinic. However, this assessment seemed different already. Mr. Cameron took a deep breath as he sat down. *I wonder where this session is headed.*

Mental Health Clinic

Although part of the Medical Center on Wright Patterson Air Force Base (WPAFB), the Mental Health Clinic (MHC) was a public facility housed in a separate building within walking distance. The building, previously a small hospital,

Development of this decision case was supported in part by the University of South Carolina College of Social Work. It was prepared solely to provide material for class discussion and not to suggest either effective or ineffective handling of the situation depicted. While based on field research regarding an actual situation, names and certain facts may have been disguised to protect confidentiality. The authors and editors wish to thank the anonymous case reporter for cooperation in making this account available for the benefit of social work students and practitioners.

had been converted into well-decorated offices. Clients were initially screened at the Medical Center before being assigned to the different branches of the medical setting such as the Mental Health Clinic.

The fifteen-member staff included three psychiatrists, four psychologists, and eight clinical social workers, with professional experience ranging from 2 to 25 years. Of the fifteen staff members, two were African-American and thirteen white; ten were male and five female. All but two were military personnel. The two civilians were psychologists. Dr. Jim Dillon, who supervised the MHC social workers, had been a clinical social worker in the Air Force for the past 20 years.

MHC maintained regular office hours from 7:30 a.m. to 4:30 p.m., and most clients scheduled appointments in advance. However, it also provided services to "walk-ins," people who came without appointments. All of the staff members at MHC were required to take their turn being "on call" to respond to such clients. Being the on–call staff member meant being physically available and prepared to provide crisis intervention, emergency psychosocial evaluations, and court-ordered assessments. There was always someone on call. The 15 staff members rotated being on call for the MHC, and each person's turn came about one day every two weeks.

Mr. Gary Cameron

Gary Cameron was 33 years old and had worked at the MHC for three years. This was his second job since completing his MSW five years earlier from the University of Illinois. Mr. Cameron had completed his BSW degree from Southern Illinois University and began a MSW program one week later. His previous job involved working with families who had mentally delayed children. His interest in working with military families came about while serving in the Air Force as an enlisted military policeman. Upon completing his four-year enlistment, he immediately began pursuing his social work education. He decided to become a social worker because of his commitment to his Christian faith. Mr. Cameron believed that the teachings of Jesus were consistent with helping others and that the social work profession was a way for him to honor God.

Mr. Gary Cameron was on call the morning Mrs. Clark came in for assistance. Since working for the MHC, Mr. Cameron had done many court-ordered assessments. The assessments usually involved three one-hour sessions to develop rapport with clients and to gather enough information to write a report with treatment recommendations for the judge ordering the assessment. This was the first time Mr. Cameron could remember doing a court-ordered assessment with a female client. All the other court-ordered assessments were with men, most of whom were referred after being convicted of driving while under the influence of drugs or alcohol.

Session One

Mr. Cameron observed Mrs. Jane Clark as she was ushered into his office. The Caucasian lady appeared to be in her 50's, was well dressed and groomed impeccably in a three-piece suit. Her hair looked like she had just been to a beautician, and she presented herself quite properly. However, she appeared distraught and upset, switching her purse from arm to arm and picking at her nails. Mr. Cameron thought he noted tears in her eyes as he stood and introduced himself.

Mrs. Clark continued to fidget with her purse as she sat down and anxiously stammered, "I have been ordered by the court to come here. I was also told that I needed an assessment as I have been accused of shoplifting at a K-Mart store." Mrs. Clark continued, "I have been married to my husband Dick for nearly 25 years. We have a good relationship even though I am concerned about his unhappiness with his job. I am not currently employed." She proceeded to explain to Mr. Cameron that they had one child, Marvin, who was a 17-year-old senior in high school. "He likes to play computer videogames in his room after school, and when he's not playing on his computer, he likes hanging around with his friends from high school." Mrs. Clark nervously cleared her throat before continuing, "Our family is a very traditional middle class family living in a middle class neighborhood of brick homes near the Air Force base. We have lived in the same three-bedroom house with an attached garage and a nice yard for eighteen years. We are just a normal family. We have no immediate family members in the area. All of our extended family members live out of state. However, we are friendly with our neighbors. I think that we have a good relationship with them."

Mr. Cameron let out a long breath and said, "Why don't you explain a little bit more in detail what brought you to the MHC and how the MHC might be of service to you."

"There is this K-Mart about one mile from my house," she explained. "I often shop there. We were planning a 'get together' with some friends and relatives who were coming from out of town over the holiday. And I was feeling a little stressed about hosting this holiday affair at our home."

"It was the middle of the afternoon, between 3:00 and 3:30 p.m., a few days before Thanksgiving," Mrs. Clark explained. "And I took a toothbrush from this store and stuck it in my purse. However, I don't remember doing it! I went out of the store not paying for it. Someone else in the store had seen me put this toothbrush in my purse. I could have paid for the toothbrush, if I really needed one, but I didn't even need one!"

Mr. Cameron thought to himself, *She was charged with shoplifting for taking a toothbrush? Why didn't the store just ask her to pay for the item?* But he asked, "Why would you have taken the toothbrush?"

"I don't know why," she responded vehemently. "I'm telling you, I don't remember. I was thinking about my plans for the holiday get together as I walked toward my car and the next thing I remember is being confronted by this security person from the store." Mrs. Clark told Mr. Cameron, "He was the one who found the toothbrush in my purse and detained me. It was the city police that took me in for questioning. They took my statement and then released me."

Mrs. Clark continued that she complied with every request of the security personnel and the police. However, she was dazed and surprised at what was happening to her. Raising her voice, Mrs. Clark repeated, "It isn't that I didn't do it. I just don't remember doing it." She paused, "What bothers me the most is having a criminal record now." Putting her head down, she added, "I've brought unnecessary embarrassment upon my family."

Mr. Cameron then asked, "Does anyone else know about this incident?"

Mrs. Clark responded, "My son and husband are the only ones that know anything about this. We agreed not to discuss this with anybody outside the family. I've never, ever done anything like this before."

Mr. Cameron asked, "How are things at home?"

"Over all, things are pretty good." Mrs. Clark commented. "Though there are some things that are causing me difficulty in my life, I love my husband and son and have high hopes for them." Mrs. Clark thought for a moment and then continued. "We have a fairly predictable routine and order to our lives. What I mean by that is that we are a family of habit; we eat at certain times, do things certain days."

Mr. Cameron then reviewed with Mrs. Clark details that he had learned about her family and the incident at K-Mart, to make sure that he understood what she had said. He said to Mrs. Clark, "It has been beneficial to hear from you directly regarding the circumstances leading to your arrest and about your family. I am looking forward to other sessions with you that would help me better understand the dilemma that you are facing."

Mrs. Clark said, "It is hard coming into an office like this and having to go over things with someone I don't even know and things I don't even remember doing. However, I appreciated the time you took, Mr. Cameron, to talk to me about the trouble I am in and about my family. It was helpful for me to finally share this information with someone like yourself."

Mr. Cameron tried to encourage Mrs. Clark, "I'm committed in assisting you through the upcoming weeks that we will be meeting."

Staffing with Dr. Dillon

Later that day Mr. Cameron discussed this case with Dr. Dillon. Mr. Cameron reported the facts of the shoplifting incident as well as Mrs. Clark's understanding and reaction to them. Dr. Dillon wondered whether Mrs. Clark had experienced a Dissociative Fugue prompted by some precipitating stressful event in her life. He suggested that Mr. Cameron read the Diagnostic and Statistical Manual of Mental Disorders, fourth edition (DSM-IV), to see whether Mrs. Clark met the criteria for a dissociative disorder. He also suggested that Mr. Cameron spend the next two sessions identifying the stressful events in her life and develop a report to the judge with a plan for effective management.

Session Two

The following Monday Mrs. Clark arrived on time but appeared anxious. She sat on the edge of her chair and clung tightly to her purse. Wanting to put her at ease, Mr. Cameron gently asked her to share about her husband.

"He retired about 15 years ago after 20 years in the Air Force. Immediately after retiring, Dick started a second career as a U.S. postal service worker." Mrs. Clark said, "I thought it would be a good career move for him. It is a stable income, and he retains his service benefits. After 20 years of service, Dick could retire and draw two pensions—one with the Air Force and a second with the postal service plus Social Security. Financially, we are doing well and are financially secure as we anticipate our retirement years."

"Dick was content with his employment until the last couple of years. Since then he has wanted to move into some other area of the postal system to get off the streets, preferably something in a supervisory capacity, but there have not been any openings. I think this has truly frustrated him; he has become very dissatisfied with his job. He now counts the days until he can retire even though he had aimed to reach the 20-year mark of retirement status. He has five years to go before he is eligible to retire." Mrs. Clark sighed. "He is so unhappy now with his job. It just eats him up inside. I hate to see him like this."

"What about your relationship with him?" Mr. Cameron asked.

"Our relationship is loving," she replied. "I'm comfortable with it. We haven't had any significant marital conflicts during our marriage." She attributed that to the fact that she does not like conflict and, for that matter, neither does her husband. Mrs. Clark described their family as "a very close-knit family, spending a lot of time at home together but each doing our own thing. Probably the closest thing we do is go out to dinner together every other Friday." She related, "But a typical evening after work and school is I get dinner ready, we eat supper, I clean up afterwards, then Dick goes off and watches some sports game, depending on the season, while I work on some kind of craft. We sit in the living room until bedtime, while Marvin goes to his room to watch TV or does something on the computer. We are just an average family."

Mrs. Clark then put her head in her hands. "But now look at the trouble I'm in. I've certainly never done anything like this before. I haven't ever been a client at the MHC before nor have I been to any other counselor."

Mr. Cameron asked, "Have you and your husband discussed the shoplifting incident anymore?"

She responded, "We haven't discussed anything. I am leaving it up to my husband to raise the subject, but he has chosen not to discuss it or ask any questions."

Mr. Cameron and Mrs. Clark then discussed during the rest of the session how Mr. Clark's job situation added stress to her life and possible ways the two of them could communicate about the pressures in their lives. Mr. Cameron spent some time after the session reviewing his notes and praying for wisdom. He decided to inquire about other stressful life events with Mrs. Clark during the next session.

Session Three

Mrs. Clark walked in the next week appearing much more at ease. She appeared calm, so Mr. Cameron decided to get to the heart of the matter. After brief preliminaries, he asked her, "What are the primary stressors in your life right now?"

"Being convicted of this crime and perhaps doing time in jail," Mrs. Clark responded immediately.

"I understand how that possibility would loom heavy on your mind, but are there any others?" Mr. Cameron probed.

"Cancer."

Mr. Cameron immediately thought about his own father who was undergoing aggressive treatment for cancer. But because this was her concern, Mr. Cameron wanted to learn more about her physical health and why she had this fear of cancer.

Initially, she responded, "I guess I'm OK, but I don't know for sure."

Mr. Cameron asked, "Why do you think you are OK but don't know for certain?"

"A little over five years ago," she began, "I was diagnosed and treated for cancer of the bladder. I went for regular visits and was on a treatment plan. They were able to get all the cancer through the various treatments I was on." Mrs. Clark explained that she took medication and had gone through a series of chemotherapy and radiation treatment sessions. However, now she was living in fear of the worst case scenario. With teary eyes, she acknowledged, "I am afraid of the possibility of the cancer returning." Holding a handkerchief, she periodically dabbed at her eyes.

Mrs. Clark related that over the last couple of years she had been involved in follow-up appointments with her doctor who thought annual checkups were adequate. These follow-up visits at the Medical Center included an invasive procedure to determine the condition of her bladder, and specifically to see if there was any cancer. As the five-year anniversary date had approached, the doctor recommended that she get a thorough checkup. Mrs. Clark said, "At this point, he has requested that I come into the office for a full-scale physical to be sure that all the cancer is gone." She informed Mr. Cameron, "The five-year point was a couple of months ago and as of today's date I have not scheduled this appointment. I'm worried about this procedure; it is just so painful, and I don't know what the reports might reveal."

Mr. Cameron asked, "What specifically are you worried about?"

She responded, "I am afraid there still might be cancer." Subsequently, Mrs. Clark disclosed that she was fearful of dying and that she equated having cancer in her system with dying.

Then Mr. Cameron asked, "Have you had any indications of its reoccurrence?"

"No," Mrs. Clark's eyes filled with tears, "I'm just afraid and don't want to go alone."

Given Mrs. Clark's worried responses to his last two questions, Mr. Cameron could identify her fears as similar to his father's fear of dying. Mr. Cameron also felt a strong desire to be helpful and asked, "What would you think of my meeting you at your appointment?" Almost immediately he wondered, *Should I have said that?* However, he couldn't take back his question so he went ahead with his first thought.

"I guess that would be OK with me," she said, apparently caught off guard by his offer.

"It won't be a problem for me," Mr. Cameron explained, "because the Hospital Center is the building right next to ours." Mr. Cameron then continued to probe a bit. "I sense that there is still something troubling you. Is there anything else you would like to share?"

Mrs. Clark hung her head for a moment, and sighed. "Well, I guess there is an issue I recently had with my son." She paused before continuing, "My son got into trouble the day before I was caught shoplifting. We had just learned that he's been taking drugs. He obtained the drugs at his school from a friend." Mrs. Clark exclaimed, "I had no idea that Marvin was even thinking about drugs, let alone experimenting with them."

Mr. Cameron nodded for her to continue.

"He was an excellent student in junior high school, but when he got to high school, I noticed a gradual deterioration of his grades. He used to get As and Bs, but now he gets Cs with a few Ds. So far, he has not failed any courses but I'm worried that he will sooner or later." She continued, "Dick also doesn't seem to care. I'm the one that has to attend the parent/teacher conferences alone. Dick just says, 'Hey, I've had a hard day at work, and I just want to stay home and rest.'"

Mrs. Clark started fidgeting with her rings. "I am sure Marvin will come to his senses. We would like to see him go to a university. We want him to attend Wright State because it's so close. We are open to him studying anything he wants, as long as he gets a college education and goes to a nearby university." Mrs. Clark said, "Marvin staying home during his four years of college sounds like a good idea to Dick and me." She assured Mr. Cameron that Marvin was "OK with the idea." As though trying to convince Mr. Cameron, she said, "Marvin is really a good boy, but I know that some of his friends have influenced him in not caring about his grades."

"Who are these friends?" Mr. Cameron asked.

"I haven't the foggiest idea who they are," Mrs. Clark shrugged. "They don't come over to the house. I think he meets with them at school functions, like dances or football games, but I'm not sure what they do together." After pausing briefly, she continued, "He's not involved in any extracurricular activities. When he comes home after school, he either plays videogames or, if the weather's nice, he goes outside and skateboards in the neighborhood. He's in his room a lot watching TV or using the computer."

Mrs. Clark volunteered, "I was the one that found out that my son was using drugs." She continued, "I am a meticulous housekeeper. One day I noticed that Marvin's room was a mess so I went into his room to rearrange and pick up things. When I opened one of his drawers I found the marijuana cigarettes. I let it go for a day or two and didn't say anything to him. On the third day I decided I had to say something to him about the drugs. When I confronted him, Marvin said, 'I was only experimenting with it. I only tried it once, last weekend.' He told me the person, a friend at school, who gave him the drugs and then promised me he would never use drugs again. I don't think he was telling me the whole truth, but that's how we left it."

"Later that evening I decided to talk to Dick about my confrontation with Marvin," Mrs. Clark said. "He listened but didn't do anything about it."

"After my discussion with Marvin and talking to my husband, I decided not to discuss this with the school personnel, as this would only bring more attention to our son. After all, he was only experimenting with it; he's not a user."

There was a brief lull in the conversation as Mrs. Clark lowered her face in apparent disappointment. She then said, "Marvin used to attend church with me and is still on the membership roll; but when he became a teenager, he gradually stopped going and now only goes to church occasionally." She continued, "I go to the First Presbyterian Church every Sunday where I am a member. I believe you should be involved in your church. Other than that I don't think our family has any other ties to our community or even to the Air Force base."

"I'm a Christian," Mrs. Clark volunteered. "I think Dick is a Christian, because he used to go to church with us and his name is still on the roll. But I'm really not sure anymore, whether he is a Christian or not." She commented, "Church is important to me. I wish that church was as important to my family as it is to me and that we could pray together."

Mr. Cameron responded, "I'm also a Christian and can identify with how important church is to you."

She asked, "Could we pray together?"

Mr. Cameron agreed to do so. But first he asked, "What would you like me to pray for?"

Mrs. Clark said, "For strength and wisdom… that I will do the things I need to do. To have a better understanding of what I didn't have before now and what would make me a stronger person and a better Christian."

Though Mrs. Clark did not pray, she smiled after the prayer and commented, "I feel more relaxed and confident that God had not abandoned me."

Hearing her comments, Mr. Cameron responded, "It seems as if prayer is important to you." He continued, "Have you considered talking with your pastor?"

"I'm too embarrassed," Mrs. Clark replied, "to talk to my pastor or anyone at church about the shoplifting incident. I suspect that some folks at church can tell something is wrong, but I am too embarrassed to explain what happened."

Mr. Cameron starting wrapping up the session by once again encouraging Mrs. Clark to schedule a follow-up evaluation with her oncologist. They also discussed what feelings she might experience depending on the outcome of the oncologist's report.

"If I get a clean bill of health," she said, "all the other things in my life will be OK; my son's drug experimentation and court findings. But if not, then nothing else will matter to me."

Because he had already committed himself to accompanying Mrs. Clark to her appointment earlier in the session, Mr. Cameron reminded her, "Let me know when you make the appointment to see the oncologist and I will make sure I meet you at office."

Apparently relieved, Mrs. Clark said as she left his office, "That would be great. I'll call you with the appointment time and meet you there!"

Writing the Court Report

As Mrs. Clark left the office, Mr. Cameron pulled out the necessary forms to write his report to the judge. Based on past experience, Mr. Cameron knew the judge would use the report when rendering a sentence for Mrs. Clark. Although Mr. Cameron had gathered a lot of information on Mrs. Clark and her family, he was uncertain about what to write. Mr. Cameron contemplated the several conflicting thoughts and emotions he was having about the assessment. *In some ways,* he thought, *Mrs. Clark should not have been charged with a crime. She's a woman in her 50s with no prior record. She only took a toothbrush that she could have easily paid for.*

Moreover, Mr. Cameron thought, *several situational stressors could have contributed to the incident occurring. She really needs support and encouragement, not the additional stress of being charged with a crime.* After stopping to pray for Mrs. Clark, he thought, *She seems genuinely remorseful for what happened. At the same time*, he thought, *justice must be done. I have to consider what is best for society and not just what is best for Mrs. Clark. In some ways, her cancer and her problems with her son don't have anything to do with her taking the toothbrush.* Staring at the paperwork, he wondered where to begin.

13

AM I MISSING SOMETHING?

Mary Anne Poe & Sherry Bell

Feeling devastated, school social worker Susan Brantley hung up the phone and contemplated her options. Most members of the Individual Education Plan (IEP) team, along with Robby Pearson and his mother, were already standing around the school's administrative office, waiting for the meeting to start. Susan felt certain that the directive she had just received from the Director of Special Education was unethical and even illegal. By law, every member of an IEP team had an independent vote. Susan sensed that what she decided in the next few minutes would live with her from that point onward as a reflection of her integrity. It also had very serious implications for Robby. *Am I missing some bit of information or insight about Robby's risk to others*, Susan wondered, *or is this a clear case of discrimination?*

The Town of Florence

Located in gently rolling James County, the town of Florence, Tennessee had a population of about 120,000. Located conveniently near an interstate highway, it had experienced significant economic and population growth in recent years. New businesses, housing developments, a new shopping mall, a new courthouse, and new churches were springing up around the area. Nevertheless, Florence struggled with overcoming racist practices of the past. The town was still mostly

Development of this decision case was supported in part by the University of South Carolina College of Social Work. It was prepared solely to provide material for class discussion and not to suggest either effective or ineffective handling of the situation depicted. While based on field research regarding an actual situation, names and certain facts may have been disguised to protect confidentiality. The authors and editors wish to thank the anonymous case reporter for cooperation in making this account available for the benefit of social work students and practitioners.

Revised from Poe, M. A., & Bell, S. (2003). Am I missing something? *Social Work & Christianity, 30*(2), 162-169. Copyright © 2003 NACSW.

segregated in terms of housing, church attendance, and social organizations. The economic development had mostly aided the predominantly white western part of town. The public education system struggled to keep up with the growth of the larger community and to overcome the problems that a history of segregation and unequal education had left behind.

The James County School System

The James County School System (JCSS) served about 18,000 children, ages three to twenty-one. There were sixteen elementary schools, four intermediate schools, five middle schools, and four high schools. The school system had about 4,200 children certified as disabled, who received special education services. These disabilities included mental retardation, learning difficulties, emotional/behavioral disturbances, and physical disabilities, such as low vision, hearing loss, speech, and mobility. About 280 students were classified as emotionally disturbed. Most of these students, about 240, were Black and had low socioeconomic status.

A White superintendent and three assistants, two of whom were White and one of whom was Black, led the system. All of the schools had a principal and an assistant principal. Guidance counselors served in each of the schools. One crisis counselor served the needs of the nine intermediate and middle schools. Two crisis counselors served the four high schools. The elementary schools did not have a crisis counselor to assist them. Two social workers, both White, served the entire system and worked only with students educationally certified as emotionally disturbed.

While the town's population was about 65% White and 35% Black, the school system was about 50% White and 50% Black. About 20% of the children in Florence attended private schools. Almost all of these students were White. This compared to about 8% as a national average for private school attendance. Perhaps this was one reason for the high percentage of children in special education in the public school system and also for the lack of community investment in high quality education. The school system had been placed under the supervision of the federal courts in 1974 as a result of a lawsuit filed and won by the NAACP. The system had made significant progress toward integrated and equal education for all according to the federal court guidelines, but the changes had sapped considerable energy from the overall education program and probably were the main reason so many White families chose to send their children to private schools.

Susan Brantley and the School System

Susan Brantley's Christian faith had given her a strong sense of commitment to advocate for at-risk children. She pursued social work education as a way to make a difference in the lives of families and children that needed help and support. Her faith bolstered her sense of justice and reinforced social work and Christian values of advocating for those with little or no power. Integrity in professional practice and following one's convictions were Susan's deeply held beliefs.

Susan earned her MSW from the University of Alabama in 1991. After graduation she provided clinical services to children and youth at Behavioral Health Services (BHS), the local hospital's behavioral and mental health unit in Tennessee. In 1993, JCSS contracted with BHS to provide social work services for emotionally disturbed students in the school system. Susan was chosen for this position and became the first social worker ever placed in the James County school system. She soon developed a caseload, providing case management services to students and their families, individual and group counseling to students, and consultation services for teachers and administrators. For five years, Susan worked full-time as an employee of BHS on a contract with the school system. She had advocated vigorously for the school system itself to hire a social worker and, in 1997, the school superintendent hired her to fill this position.

In 1998, the school superintendent, in consultation with Susan and the Director of Special Education, hired a second social worker. This social worker replaced Susan in providing direct counseling services so that Susan could be an administrator responsible for overseeing self-contained classrooms in nine different schools for emotionally disturbed (ED) students, providing in-service training to all special education teachers, and serving as a consultant to all schools who served ED students. She also developed and became the administrator of the day treatment program for the most severely mentally ill or at-risk students.

Susan's supervisor was Pamela Hutchens, the Director of Special Education for the school system. They had been friends in this community for many years and attended church together. Susan's social work values had conflicted on one occasion in the past with what Pamela wanted her to do. But they had been able to resolve this without too much difficulty. Susan understood the complexity of Pamela's responsibility to manage all the special education services. For her part, Pamela generally allowed Susan to do her job without infringing on Susan's professional judgment. Susan knew that Pamela respected her strong convictions to advocate for the children in her care.

Some staff perceived the children who Susan served as the most undesirable students in the schools, even dangerous and unfit for the public education setting. But Susan felt a special calling by God to serve these particular young people and their families. She had been blessed by their achievements and strengthened by the courage and perseverance that they and their families often demonstrated. She took seriously her advocacy role in an environment where some preferred to segregate, or put out of public view, the realities of their existence and the extent of support they needed to be successful.

Robby Pearson's Story

Robby Pearson was born with cerebral palsy. The left side of his body was partially paralyzed and very weak. He was not confined to a wheelchair, but he walked with a noticeable limp. He was very small compared to all his classmates. He also had a pronounced speech impediment, making him very hard to understand in conversation. Robby's previous schools had provided a variety of special services, including speech, physical, and occupational therapy.

In 1997, when Robby was seven years old and in the second grade, he and his family moved to Florence and the James County School System. Soon after school began, Robby's teachers asked for additional assessments because of his aggressive and impulsive behavior in class. He was diagnosed with Attention Deficit/ Hyperactive Disorder and Ritalin was prescribed. Later that year he was also diagnosed with Intermittent Explosive Disorder. He was placed for the first time in a self-contained ED class, one of the few White students in this class. Susan became his social worker and provided individual and group counseling to him. Over time she learned to know him and his family very well.

Through Susan's counseling with Robby, she came to see that Robby's home had multiple problems. He was the oldest of three children, all boys. His parents divorced when Robby was nine years old. His father moved away and failed to maintain contact with him. The mother had a string of boyfriends in the following year, several of whom were abusive to Robby and his siblings. She worked nights as a topless waitress and was often unavailable during the days or evenings when the children needed supervision. Not surprising to Susan, Robby did not do well at school and made very little progress.

Susan watched Robby's world rapidly deteriorate during his fifth grade year.

She had to report Robby's mother to the Department of Children's Services due to the abuse and neglect that she suspected. Everyone agreed that Robby could move in with his grandmother, and the Department of Children's Services recommended that Robby be placed in her custody rather than their own. Robby's mother visited sporadically and under the supervision of his grandmother. This gave him a much more stable home environment.

His behavior at school became more appropriate. He was no longer aggressive and by the end of his fifth grade year, the IEP team decided that he no longer needed special education classes for the emotionally disturbed. In sixth through eighth grades, Robby worked well in regular classroom settings. He was excited as high school approached and the prospect of moving to a new school was a welcome challenge.

Just a few months before he was to begin high school, however, Robby experienced the death of his grandmother and returned to his mother's still unstable home. He got into a physical altercation with her at home and was again removed from her care. He was placed for a few weeks at Springside Youth Home (SYH), a residential treatment program for young people, before returning to his mother with an array of supportive services for the home.

The IEP Meeting

Robby's school sent his records to the new high school he would attend the following fall. This was the normal routine for all students promoted to high school. The lead special education teacher in the school would review the special education records and arrange the necessary IEP meetings. Susan was routinely invited to every IEP meeting for students with ED certification. Others invited to this meeting would include Mr. McCall, the new high school principal who was Black, an attorney with the Department for Children's Services, an education consultant for the Department of Children's Services, a special education teacher, a regular education teacher at the high school, Robby, and his mother. Susan had been a part of many IEP meetings for Robby in their eight-year relationship. Because he had been doing so well in school, she assumed this one would be routine as they considered his beginning in high school and the appropriate placement for him.

The lead teacher called Susan a few days prior to the IEP meeting. She reported, "Mr. McCall wants Robby in the ED class. He read the records and doesn't want to take a chance."

"But he's had no problems," Susan responded with a bit of surprise, "it's been years since he had a problem!"

"I know. I agree with you," the teacher said. "He ought to have a chance."

"I am so disappointed. That's not right," Susan declared.

"I know, Robby's mother wants him in a regular class, too. So does Robby. She thinks it's not fair. I talked with her this morning. She thinks he will have a lot more trouble if he is not in a regular class. He'll be mad."

"I would be mad, too." Susan replied. "I'm gonna have to think about this. I'm gonna have to support Robby here. He's done so well. We've got to give him a chance. He's done okay—actually really good in school."

"I know. I know," the teacher said, "but I'm in a tough place. I've gotta support McCall. He is adamant. Sorry."

"Thanks for giving me the heads up on this. See you on Thursday," Susan said, ending the phone conversation.

Susan knew the special ed teacher understood that parents have considerable legal power in IEP meetings. Parents can state what they want for their child and if school personnel disagree, the school must go through a legal proceeding called due process in order to overrule the parent's wishes.

I guess I need to call Pamela on this one, Susan thought to herself. *Just to let her know what is happening.* She went ahead and dialed Pamela's number while it was on her mind. She explained to Pamela her reasoning concerning Robby's placement, the principal's position and the family's wishes. Pamela told Susan, "You vote your conscience in the meeting. It's okay. That's your job. It seems to me, too, that this kid ought to have a chance."

Susan felt relieved. At least her supervisor would back her up. Susan and Pamela discussed briefly the legal and ethical ramifications of this case. Susan was all set for the meeting, even though she always regretted having to disagree with others on the team. She felt positive about her support for Robby and about his capabilities to perform well in a regular classroom.

Susan arrived at the school in time to talk with the principal in his office a few minutes before the meeting. She wanted to have a private conversation with him to voice her disagreement with his plan to place Robby in an ED class. She did not want to catch him off-guard with her recommendation.

Susan said to him, "Mr. McCall, I know you're concerned about Robby's behavior, but he has done so well—three years of doing okay. I understand your concerns, I don't mean any disrespect for you, but I have to vote for what I think is best for the student. I just wanted you to know before the meeting."

"I know, I know. You're supposed to be for the student," he replied, "but I just can't take a chance on this one. Let him start in the ED class and see how he does here first. Thanks for coming by. I'll be at the meeting in a minute."

After meeting with him, Susan reflected on her history with the school system. *I've not had many occasions to go against the principals or teachers,* Susan thought. *I have to put the student first, though. That's the social worker's responsibility. I've got to go on into that meeting, even if McCall doesn't like my position.*

As Susan, Robby, his mother, and the legal advocate waited in the meeting room for the whole IEP team to gather, the school secretary came to get Susan, "You've got a phone call. It's Pamela. She says it's an emergency." Susan left the meeting room and went to the office to answer the phone. She had to take the phone in the office area where the principal's assistant and a few others were present. Robby and his mother followed her and waited outside the office. When Susan picked up the phone receiver, she could hardly believe Pamela's words.

"Don't go into that meeting, Susan," Pamela insisted.

"What? Why not?" Susan responded with surprise.

"The super just called. He told me that my staff COULD NOT vote against a principal and he was talking about Robby's case."

"Pamela, I'm willing to suffer the consequences. I know he'll be mad, but . . ."

"Susan, you can't go in," Pamela cut her off. "It's both our jobs. He told me to manage my staff and that school personnel should support one another. Else it's insubordination. That's the word he used."

Susan could not talk freely to Pamela in the office setting. She ended the conversation quickly. "Well, okay, bye, I'll talk to you later."

Susan could hardly believe that her supervisor and the superintendent were asking her to do something so blatantly unethical and even illegal. By law, every member of an IEP team has an independent vote. *Besides that, I'm a Christian. I can't just not go. How can Pamela ask me to do this?* Susan wondered. She had a huge dilemma now. They were not supporting her legal right, were even encouraging her to violate a professional ethical mandate to advocate for her clients, and it violated her faith, too. What was she going to do? All these people were standing around the office. Susan paused a moment to think through her options before turning to face the others. *Should I just leave the building? What do I say to Robby and his mother? What should I say to others if I just leave? Should I defy the school superintendent, go back in and vote my conscience? Are there other options?*

14

THE ELIGIBILITY ERROR

Mackenzi Huyser & Terry A. Wolfer

Social worker Sarah Adams wrung her hands as she paced up and down the hall outside of supervisor Rochelle Robinson's office. Rochelle was just finishing a phone call and had asked Sarah to wait outside before they began their weekly Friday afternoon supervision session. Sarah couldn't stop thinking about what had happened that morning with Ms. Washington. She also knew Rochelle would ask about the families who participated in the orientation session last Saturday. What should I say? Sarah wondered. I know Rochelle will be able to tell that something is wrong with me. Should I tell her what I found out?

Fort Wayne, Indiana

Located in the northeast corner of Indiana, Fort Wayne was a mid-size metropolitan area with a population of approximately 500,000 in the city and surrounding areas. Approximately 200,000 residents lived within the city limits. Like many other cities, Fort Wayne experienced a rapid growth in suburbanization in the 1950s and 1960s. As a result, fewer economic resources were available in the city, impacting residents, housing stock, the city tax base, and social service programs.

Social service housing organizations in Fort Wayne included both those that provided housing services and those that provided housing resources. Housing service organizations included Habitat for Humanity Fort Wayne, a local affiliate of Habitat

Development of this decision case was supported in part by the University of South Carolina College of Social Work. It was prepared solely to provide material for class discussion and not to suggest either effective or ineffective handling of the situation depicted. While based on field research regarding an actual situation, names and certain facts may have been disguised to protect confidentiality. The authors wish to thank the anonymous case reporter for cooperation in making this account available for the benefit of social work students and practitioners.

for Humanity International, and New Hope Housing Corporation. New Hope offered services ranging from affordable housing to home ownership programs. Like other housing service organizations, New Hope actually housed people through emergency shelter services or other housing in the community. Housing resource organizations, in constrast, provided advocacy for housing policy issues or funding to housing service organizations. The Indiana Planning Council on the Homeless and the United Way of Allen County were two such organizations.

New Hope Housing Corporation

New Hope was established in 1980 as a non-profit faith-based organization. Located in the heart of Fort Wayne, the mission of the organization was to "serve individuals, families, and communities through innovative housing programs as a response to God's call for social justice." New Hope had built a solid reputation in the community based in part on this commitment to social justice.

New Hope had strong leadership. It was headed by the Jon Powell, a dynamic leader who had served as Executive Director since 1990. He held a Master of Social Work degree and had received an honorary doctorate degree from a local university. His vision and leadership were an important part of the positive reputation New Hope held in the community. In addition to Powell's leadership, the 15-member Board of Directors also promoted the mission and vision of the organization through strategic collaboration with external organizations. Board members served three-year terms and were well-respected community members. They brought to the organization a willingness to work, which also contributed to the strong reputation the organization held in the community.

New Hope offered a number of housing opportunities in the community, including emergency shelter services, rental properties, assisted living facilities, a home ownership program, and a loan assistance program. Together, these programs served nearly 200 families each year, 70% of which were female-headed households. Twenty staff members implemented the programs. Staff members came from various educational backgrounds, with most holding Bachelor of Social Work or Sociology degrees. Seven staff members also held Master of Social Work degrees.

New Hope relied on multiple funding streams. It received a significant portion of its funding from Christian churches and individual donors. In addition, the organization pursued and won many foundation grants, and funding from the state and federal governments. A close connection with the city of Fort Wayne also allowed the organization to purchase vacant homes in the central city for back taxes, thus allowing the organization to spend money on renovations rather than pay full cost for these structures.

Sarah Adams

Sarah Adams, a Caucasian female, graduated in 1997 from a small Christian college in Michigan with a Bachelor's degree in Sociology. As a teen, she had developed a strong passion for urban and community issues through volunteer work, so decided to focus her attention on community development. In this program she was able to take some social work courses, and also focus on macro issues in the community.

After graduating she moved to Fort Wayne. She took a job at Central City Homeless Shelter as a day program assistant. She was directly involved with organizing day programs for the mostly male residents, which included job training and life skills development. She initially enjoyed this position and the opportunities to develop activities for the residents, but felt herself being worn down from the residents' limited progress. Month after month, she would see the same clients and help them with the same skills. Her work didn't seem to make a difference.

After three years at the homeless shelter, Sarah felt a need for change. She was anxious to learn more about program administration and decided to enroll in a Master of Social Work program. It would be too expensive, she decided, to enroll in the program full-time without being able to supplement her expenses with a steady income, so she decided to start as a part-time student and seek a change in employment.

Her job search did not last long; she heard of an opening at New Hope's home ownership program and applied immediately. She knew about this program from previous volunteer work with Habitat for Humanity and strongly believed in their mission. She interviewed for and was offered the position of case manager in the home ownership program. Part of her role would be to implement a new pilot program New Hope was starting with the Department of Housing and Urban Development (HUD). This yearlong pilot program would assist families receiving Section 8 assistance with a transition to home ownership through New Hope's preexisting home ownership program. HUD paid New Hope to recruit families into this new program and for program costs associated with serving these families. In collaboration with New Hope staff, HUD developed the eligibility guidelines for the Section 8 families that would be part of the HUD/New Hope partnership program and polices to guide its implementation. HUD administrators and New Hope staff were eager to determine the success of the partnership program and hoped it would continue as a permanent program following the pilot year.

Saturday Morning

Sarah arrived at the New Hope office at 7:55 a.m. on an April Saturday morning. She and Eliza Brown, a social work colleague, would be leading a home ownership information session. They had led sessions together before and were comfortable with the material they needed to present.

All clients interested in New Hope's home ownership program were required to attend an information session. New Hope offered the information session every six weeks on a Saturday from 8:30 a.m. to 5:00 p.m., and provided lunch and childcare to families who pre-registered.

On this day, fifteen families had pre-registered, an average turnout for a spring information session. New Hope had seen a marked increase in their client numbers since they began the pilot HUD/New Hope partnership program.

"Looks like we're all set up," Eliza said as she filled the last information packet with a brochure describing the home ownership program.

"Okay," Sarah replied, "I'll unlock the doors and we can start with registration."

As Sarah opened the door, the first participant greeted her for the information session.

"Good morning," the African American woman said.

"Good morning," Sarah replied, "my name is Sarah, and I'm a case manager here in the home ownership program."

"Hello Ms. Sarah, my name is Ms. Washington," the woman volunteered, "I'm here for the information session."

"Welcome! We're meeting in the last room on the right," Sarah pointed down the hall. "We have coffee and donuts available and Eliza, one of the other case managers in our program, will help you register."

"Thank you," Ms. Washington said as she walked down the hall.

Twenty minutes later all the pre-registered participants had arrived and checked in and Sarah began the session.

"On behalf of the New Hope Housing Corporation, Eliza and I would like to welcome you to our home ownership program information session," Sarah said.

"The participants, all of whom were female, sat in a circle listening intently.

"Why don't we start by introducing ourselves," Sarah continued. "If you would like, please tell your name, and perhaps how you heard about New Hope and the home ownership program."

The women began, saying only a few things about themselves, their name, whether they had children, and why they were interested in the home ownership program. Sarah knew from experience it usually took until at least lunchtime for the participants to feel comfortable enough to really engage in the session. Five of the women, including Ms. Washington, were currently receiving Section 8 assistance and were possible candidates for the pilot HUD/New Hope partnership program.

The information session continued with both Sarah and Eliza leading portions of the session on topics such as financial credit, budgeting, insurance, and other key issues the families would learn throughout the three year program.

At four o'clock the women were asked, if they remained interested in the program, to complete the application sheets in their information packets. Sarah and Eliza walked around the room to assist the women with their applications.

At the end of the session, thirteen women left completed applications. Later, Sarah and Eliza divided the applications among themselves and arranged follow-up appointments with the women.

Wednesday Morning

"Good morning," Sarah said, and asked the man who answered the telephone, "May I speak with Ms. Washington?"

"Who's calling?" the man asked, sounding suspicious.

"This is Sarah Adams, from New Hope Housing Corporation. Ms. Washington..."

"Just a minute," the man interrupted.

Sarah waited, wondering what kind of family situation she was dealing with. *Could this man be Ms. Washington's brother? He didn't sound old enough to be her uncle or father.*

"Hello, this is Ms. Washington," a voice broke in on Sarah's thoughts.

"Hello, Ms. Washington, this is Sarah Adams calling from New Hope Housing Corporation. We met at the information session on Saturday." Sarah continued,

"I'm reviewing your application materials and wonder if we could set up an appointment to go over your current situation."

"That would be fine," Ms. Washington said, "I leave for work at 2:00 p.m. each day, so anytime in the morning would be fine."

"That would be great. Could we meet this Friday at 9:00 a.m.?" Sarah questioned.

"Yes, that works, I will see you then," Ms. Washington said and she hung up the telephone.

Friday Morning

"This seems to be moving quickly," Ms. Washington said as she sat down in Sarah's office to discuss her completed application.

"We're trying to focus our efforts on applicants currently receiving Section 8 for our pilot program," Sarah explained, "and your application seems very strong. Perhaps we could start with you telling me about your interest in this pilot partnership program."

"When I moved here last year from Illinois," Ms. Washington explained, "I became interested in home ownership. I began exploring what programs offered and thought this program seemed like a good option, especially because of the transition from Section 8 to home ownership. I learned a lot about home ownership at the information session and would like to see if I can eventually own my own home."

"Well," Sarah said, "from my review of your application it seems like you would be a good fit for the program. Let's go ahead and review some of this information from your application to see what areas need focus in the next couple of months." Scanning the application, Sarah continued, "It looks like you transferred your Section 8 benefits from Illinois. Is that correct?"

"Yes," Ms. Washington explained, "we moved here to be closer to my parents."

"Okay," Sarah said, "and you have three daughters, two of whom live with you in your current place?"

Ms. Washington nodded and Sarah continued.

"You work second shift at Strong Packaging Company," Sarah confirmed. "Have you been full-time since you moved here?"

"Yes," Ms. Washington said, "I just started my tenth month."

Sarah continued, "And your annual income is $23,000?"

Ms. Washington nodded.

"Any other household income?" Sarah asked, thinking of the many families in the home ownership program who often supplemented their employment wages by babysitting during a shift they were not working.

"My husband makes $42,000 a year," Ms. Washington reported in a matter of fact tone.

"Your husband?" Sarah questioned, surprised this information hadn't been reported on Ms. Washington's application.

"Yes," Ms. Washington explained, "he works two jobs, second shift during the week, and another job part-time on the weekends."

Sarah thought for a moment. She wasn't completely sure of the income eligibility guidelines for Section 8, but this didn't seem right. *What's her total household income?* Sarah wondered, and began mental calculations.

"Your household income is over $60,000 a year," Sarah exclaimed.

"Yes, does that make us ineligible for the home ownership program?" Ms. Washington asked.

"Yes," Sarah stated. "We work with families who are receiving Section 8 assistance or who have household incomes between $30,000 and $45,000 per year."

"Well," Ms. Washington responded, "I still fall in that category."

"You would," Sarah said, "but you just said you were married and you and your husband's income combined put you over the income eligibility. Why are you receiving Section 8 assistance?"

"Because of my income," Ms. Washington explained.

"Does your Section 8 case worker know you are married and that your husband also contributes to your household income?" Sarah asked.

"I don't know," Ms. Washington said, appearing irritated. "Why don't you just tell me what programs you have that I am eligible to receive?"

Looking at Ms. Washington, Sarah thought about the clients who so badly needed housing assistance such as Section 8. She opened her desk file and pulled out an information sheet on the New Hope's loan assistance program.

"You are eligible for a low-interest loan that will assist you in buying a home," Sarah said flatly. "You are welcome to take this sheet home and review it. I could also give you the application materials for this program."

"I will take a look at that and call you if I need an application," Ms. Washington said as she stood up and walked out the door.

Sarah stood up, moved to her office door, and watched as Ms. Washington brushed past the receptionist and walked out of the office.

"What was that all about?" Eliza questioned as she passed Sarah's office.

Sarah shook her head and moved back to her desk. As she sat and thought about the appointment she grew more and more frustrated. *What right did this woman have to receive assistance? What about all those families she had worked with over the last nine months, many of whom so desperately needed help? The waiting list for families to receive Section 8 assistance was nearly two years long.*

Friday Afternoon

"Come on in, Sarah," Rochelle said after she hung up the phone.

Sarah walked into Rochelle's office, trying to compose herself.

"How's it going?" Rochelle questioned.

"Okay," Sarah replied, still not sure how or whether she should bring up the situation.

"How was the information session last weekend?" Rochelle asked.

"It went fine," Sarah answered tersely. "We had a good group."

Rochelle looked at Sarah inquiringly. Sarah could tell she knew something was wrong.

"Did you get any applications for the HUD/New Hope partnership program?" Rochelle asked.

"We got five. I took three and Eliza has the other two," Sarah replied.

"Okay," Rochelle continued slowly, "I'm heading to HUD on Monday for our nine-month pilot discussion. Any issues with these new applications I should mention?"

Sarah paused, still frustrated about Ms. Washington, and wondered, *What should I say?*

15

AIDING OR ABETTING ABORTION?

Jeanette Ucci & Terry A. Wolfer

"You aren't goin' to leave me, are you?" Cali Nelson called out plaintively.

The waiting room of the Planned Parenthood surgery clinic was full but the mood subdued. Throughout the room, young women shuffled noisily through pages of well-worn women's magazines, pretending not to pay attention. An older man stared with too much intensity at a picture taken of the ground breaking ceremony for the clinic. A young couple in the far corner made no effort to avert their attention. They just stared, waiting. Really, everyone was waiting.

I'm a social work STUDENT! Erika Burkholdt tried to sort through her thoughts. *I certainly don't want to disappoint a client. She's counting on me. This is what self-determination is all about, isn't it? Besides my field instructor asked me to be here and I agreed. How can I back out now? How can I not follow through?*

Erika saw the nurse shift her position, but it was not an impatient gesture. Cali started rocking as she stood by the door waiting for Erika to join her. "Come on. Let's go!" Cali said loudly enough to startle a woman sitting nervously next to the door.

Oh, God, Erika thought to herself, *I just don't know what to do. What's the right thing to do?*

Kansas City, Missouri

Located in western Missouri across the Missouri River from Kansas, Kansas

Development of this decision case was supported in part by the University of South Carolina College of Social Work. It was prepared solely to provide material for class discussion and not to suggest either effective or ineffective handling of the situation depicted. While based on field research regarding an actual situation, names and certain facts may have been disguised to protect confidentiality. The authors and editors wish to thank the anonymous case reporter for cooperation in making this account available for the benefit of social work students and practitioners.

City was a sprawling city of about 440,000 people. Its population was approximately 60% Caucasian, 31% African American, 2% Asian and 7% Latino. The Caucasian population was predominantly middle-class, and there was a definitive line between the haves and have-nots.

A solid Midwestern kind of city, Kansas City nevertheless included a red light district. But the district was understated compared to most such areas. The prostitutes did not dress in provocative clothing. No one stood conspicuously on a street corner or strutted around the block. Nothing was that obvious. The women and men engaging in prostitution were typically dressed in ordinary clothing and their behavior was equally ordinary. Still, many of them were addicted to crack.

New Way-Kansas City

New Way-Kansas City (New Way-KC) was a faith-related organization with offices throughout the Midwest. New Way-KC's main office was located in an old nine-story hospital building, and surrounded by working-class African American neighborhoods. The main office sat about five minutes from the red light district and a strip of the downtown area where gay and transgendered men were prevalent. New Way-KC also operated from two additional smaller buildings in the community.

In other cities, most New Way program directors were ordained ministers and New Way employees were devout Christians who took a "faith first" approach to provision of social services. New Way-KC was the exception. The Executive Director of New Way-KC was a professional administrator who provided oversight to direct service providers at many different divisional programs based outside of Kansas City. The Director hired social service professionals who did not necessarily take a faith-first approach to services.

The organizational and cultural difference between New Way-KC and other New Way facilities was sometimes a point of contention. For example, New Way-KC had won the New Way Excellence Award in 1995. However, the Executive Director of New Way had received several letters of protest from other New Way facilities, because New Way-KC's programs were sometimes staffed by professionals who were less overtly religious. Some of the letters had suggested, "They shouldn't have won because their staff are not religious or spiritual enough."

In 1996, Murray Pendergast was the head of the Social Service Division at New Way-KC. Pendergast, who was working toward a PhD in social work, had worked for New Way for many years, and had been instrumental in establishing many of the social programs there.

Pendergast supervised three directors: Molly Shaw, Director of Youth and Family Programs (YFP); Amy Landon, Director of Homeless Programs; and Margarite Pittman, Director of Senior Programs. YFP housed a variety of programs including Quick Start (an educational program for pre-school children), Open Door (a residential program for pregnant teens), Homebuilding (a family preservation program that intervened with abusive families in the community), Safe Haven (a counseling and housing program for homeless women and abused and neglected children), and the Lighthouse Program (designed to help men and women and their children through the process of coming out of prostitution.). The Homeless Programs provided food, housing, and other types of material assistance. The Senior Program provided housing for senior citizens throughout Kansas City. All of these programs were staffed by professionals, and most of the staff had either an MSW or a master's degree in another human service field. Outside of the Social Service Department, however, most New Way social programs typically employed only a few professionals and more paraprofessionals.

In general, staff members of the social service programs believed that high level administrators did not truly understand the nature of the work that the social service staff members performed. They sometimes said half-jokingly, "Oh, those administrators upstairs, they don't really know what we do down here." The numerous programs at New Way-KC operated almost like separate agencies, with each program having its own budget.

The Lighthouse Program

During the summer of 1996, the Lighthouse Program had three staff members. The Program Director was Stacey Dalpaz. Tammy Thomas was the case manager, and Erika Burkholdt was an MSW student completing a block field placement at Lighthouse, following her first year of full-time coursework.

The program was initially established in 1987 by an Episcopal congregation but New Way-KC assumed leadership in 1989 due to financial difficulties and neighborhood safety concerns at the founding church. When New Way took over the program, they fired the director, who had been quite popular with the program's clients. This caused considerable discontent among some clients.

Approximately one-third of Lighthouse's $100,000 annual program budget was funded through Kansas City United Way. A private, anonymous donor provided about $50,000, and New Way provided approximately $15,000. These contributions were highly valued because many funders were hesitant to support programs associated with prostitution, even if the goal was to help clients find alternatives to sex work. Lighthouse paid rent to New Way for its operating space. The Lighthouse staff had access to a van and some agency cars that New Way owned.

Many of the program's clients had initially been recruited through a weekly treatment group that the staff members offered in a Kansas City prison. Lighthouse was one of the first programs in the Kansas City area to bring such groups into prisons. The group, jokingly dubbed "the ho group" by participants, was designed specifically for men and women who had engaged in prostitution. The group's purpose was to help the members get out of prostitution. Nearly 90% of the clients of the Lighthouse Program were women, and many of the male clients were gay. The program staff provided case management services for clients (and their children) so that when they left prison, they would have housing, substance abuse treatment, counseling, and other supportive services. The rest of New Way staff viewed Lighthouse as the "weird" program in New Way, or "the odd child in the bunch." The Lighthouse staff thus believed that it was best just to keep to themselves.

Stacey Dalpaz, MSW, Director of Lighthouse Program

Since earning her MSW, Stacey Dalpaz had worked 12 years in sexual trauma services. Energetic and idealistic, Stacey was very committed to her job as supervisor of the Lighthouse Program. As the founding supervisor, she had begun with no staff members and carried all of the work of the program single-handedly for one year. She seemed to go out of her way for clients, often providing them with her home phone number so that they could get in touch with her at any time, if needed. Stacey often worked 6 or 7 days per week, and spent many late evenings at the Lighthouse office as well. At times, she would become very ill, missing work for about a week at a time. She had been diagnosed with lupus. Stacey was known to drop everything in order to assist a client. Her dedication was evident in the positive things that many clients said about her work.

Stacey had many professional and personal strengths. She could see the positive side of almost any client or situation, and would not refuse services to potential clients. This was especially true of former Lighthouse clients who had relapsed and now were in need of services again. She was willing to work with clients on whatever difficulties they were experiencing, and assisted them in identifying their strengths. She was open to discussing spiritual issues with clients, if this was important to them, and went out of her way to learn about types of spirituality that were unfamiliar to her. Stacey was also quite receptive to suggestions from her student intern, Erika Burkholdt.

Erika Burkholdt

A 25-year-old Caucasian woman, Erika Burkholdt had earned her undergraduate degree in Sociology from Benedictine College in Atchison, Kansas. Her undergraduate program had been unique in that the student-faculty ratio was only 16 to 1, faculty taught all courses, and students had an opportunity to develop projects and work directly with a faculty member to complete the project. The liberal-minded climate at Benedictine College mostly appealed to Erika but contrasted with her traditional Catholic upbringing. Following graduation, Erika had worked for two years as a Life Skills Trainer at a non-profit home for juvenile boys in a small town in Missouri.

In August of 1996, Erika began a field placement following completion of her foundation-level MSW coursework at the University of Missouri at Columbia. She interviewed with Amy Landon at New Way-KC, and was told that she would be assigned to the Lighthouse Program. Erika knew that she would be working with women and men (and their children) who were getting out of prostitution.

When Erika began her field placement at Lighthouse, she received little orientation during her first week. However, she was excited about working with a new and challenging population, and took the opportunity to jump right into things. She quickly noted the absence of a filing system and intake forms, and began by putting together a data sheet that she could subsequently use for intakes.

A Morning Telephone Call

On a Wednesday morning in late August, Erika was still at home getting ready for her third day of placement when the telephone rang at about 8:45 a.m. It was Stacey, Erika's supervisor from Lighthouse.

"Good morning, Erika. This is Stacey. Listen, I have an assignment for you that I wanted to get to you now because I'll be out of the office this morning. I need you to go by and pick up Cali Nelson at her home this morning at 9:30. Do you remember, she's that client I mentioned yesterday? Cali has an abortion scheduled at Planned Parenthood this morning at 10:00, and it turns out that I can't take her. You can stop by the office and get the agency car. Cali lives at 135 Hamilton Street."

"Okay, Stacey . . .," Erika responded tentatively.

"Thanks, Erika. This is a big help. It's really important."

Hanging up the phone, Erika wondered whether student interns typically received this type of task during their first week of placement. Still, she did not want to disappoint Stacey, and figured that perhaps this must be normal.

Although she had not yet met Cali Nelson, Erika remembered what Stacey had mentioned about her the day before: Cali was a 33-year-old Caucasian woman who had been a client of the Lighthouse Program for several months. She had two children—a 7-year-old daughter and a 3-year-old son—and lived with her husband. He had reportedly thrown her out of the house several times for using drugs but had taken her back in each time. Cali had a history of prostitution, had been incarcerated, and was addicted to crack. She was now 6 months pregnant with her third child. Stacey suspected that Cali had gotten pregnant from her crack dealer rather than her husband. Stacey had also mentioned that Cali sometimes mistreated her daughter. Nevertheless, Stacey believed that Cali was very intelligent, and would have had a lot going for herself, had she not become addicted to crack.

As she finished getting ready and then got into her car and drove to the Lighthouse office, Erika felt slightly nervous. *This is my first time going to pick up a client by myself,* she realized. *I've never met Cali. I wonder what she'll be like.*

In the car, Erika's thoughts soon turned more somber, *I can't believe I'm doing this. A fetus is a baby, and abortion is killing. This is absolutely crazy. Why did Stacey put me in this situation? Well, I guess I'm just giving her a ride, though,* Erica rationalized. *I remember Stacey said yesterday that she does all the counseling for clients, so I guess that would include any type of abortion counseling. Still, though, I really don't want to do this, but I can't say no to Stacey either. I don't really have a choice.*

Arriving at the Lighthouse office, Erika saw that there was no one else there. She went downstairs to check out the keys to the New Way car, and then went outside to find it.

I've never been in this position before. I mean, should I really be helping someone to get an abortion? As Erika weaved through traffic, thoughts cluttered her mind. *I'm just not sure how I feel about this. But I guess if Stacey said to, this must be typical at Lighthouse.*

Erika was thankful that she knew about where Hamilton Street was located, and calculated in her mind how to get there. She drove through the city to Hamilton Street, and parked in front of the building labeled 135. The house was a large dilapidated gray structure. *This place looks like it could blow over any second if a high wind hit it*, Erika thought nervously as she walked up to the front door. Through the closed door, Erika heard a woman hollering. When she knocked, the hollering stopped and a woman, dressed in a bathrobe, answered the door. The woman had apparently been hollering as she struggled to dress a young girl who stood next to her.

"Good morning." Momentarily startled because the woman looked twenty years older than she expected, Erika asked, "Are you Ms. Nelson?"

"Yeah, that's me," the woman responded, and resumed dressing the child.

"I'm Erika Burkholdt, from Lighthouse. Stacey Dalpaz called me this morning to come and give you a ride to the doctor's . . ."

"Yup," Cali interrupted, nodding in recognition. "I've got an appointment over there this morning. Just give me a minute to finish getting ready, and then I'll be right out."

"Okay," Erika nodded, "I'll be in the car." Before turning to walk down the porch steps, Erika noted that the house was in disarray. There was an unmade bed in the middle of the living room, and Cali's raised voice now mixed with fresh cries from the child.

Several minutes later, Cali came out of the house, and got into the car with Erika. "How's Stacey doing?" Cali asked. "Boy, I just love her. Thank God for Stacey. What would I ever do without her? Thank God for Lighthouse, giving me a ride to Planned Parenthood."

Glancing sideways, Erika noted that Cali's whole body trembled as she spoke, and she rocked back and forth in the car seat. Cali spoke rapidly, and her thoughts seemed scattered.

I wonder if she's high right now? Erika wondered warily. *At least she's not being aggressive.*

As Cali talked excitedly about Stacey and the Lighthouse, Erika's thoughts drifted. *Even though I was raised to believe that abortion is killing, I know that I'm pro-choice. People don't have any business telling other people how to run their lives. But I would never have an abortion myself. So why am I helping Cali to get one now, I mean, if this is killing a baby? Or is this just fostering Cali's right to self-determination?*

Realizing that she was unsure of the final turns to Planned Parenthood, Erika asked Cali, "Um, how do we get there now?"

Cali motioned her through several turns, and soon they were approaching the Planned Parenthood office. Erika saw that there were several picketers lined up outside the office.

"Hurry, we gotta run past those people!" Cali said excitedly as Erika parked the car.

Oh, crap, Erika thought. *I hope they don't see me.* Erika had begun to feel increasingly conflicted during the car ride, and this was making things worse.

As Erika and Cali walked across the parking lot, the picketers yelled at them, "You're gonna burn in hell, you baby killers!"

I'm totally embarrassed to be here, Erika thought. *Maybe they think I'm having an abortion. This completely goes against my beliefs, like I'm some kind of a hypocrite.*

Although Cali seemed to ignore the picketers, Erika could not. *Gosh, they're sure making this worse, for us and anyone else. Even though I don't want to be here, women shouldn't be harassed like this. This is already a hard enough decision for women who need to be here. Anyway, it's not like those signs will change anybody's mind.*

As they walked into the building together, Erika thought, *I'm really not sure that I want to be doing this.*

Obviously familiar with the agency, Cali stepped up to the reception window and spoke to the woman behind the desk. "I'm here for my abortion," she began, with what seemed to Erika like unnecessary loudness, "got a 10:00 o'clock appointment."

As Cali continued speaking loudly to the receptionist, Erika began to feel embarrassed about her tone of voice. After they were sent to the waiting room, Cali continued speaking to Erika and anyone else who would listen.

Erika tried to listen, but she was embarrassed by Cali, and her own thoughts were racing. *I mean, yes, I AM pro-choice, but yet I've always known that I would never have an abortion myself . . . And now here I am, helping someone to get an abortion, I mean, I just don't know if I feel right about this. . . . This seems like a big deal, I just don't know."*

As she pondered the situation, Erika wished for some way to separate herself from Cali's action. *I really don't feel comfortable going into the back with her when she actually has the abortion*, Erika thought. *It just doesn't feel right to me, being here at all. Maybe it is right, but I just can't do that. On the other hand, I'm a student and a responsible person, so if Stacey's told me to do this, I guess I should do it. I don't want to disappoint her the very first week of my internship. What kind of a first impression would that be? And if this is in my internship description, then I should do it, I guess.* Then Erika realized, *but I really have no idea what my job description is anyway . . . maybe this is what a social worker should be doing for a client . . . but for me personally, I'm just not sure if I should be supporting someone who's getting an abortion.*

At that point, Erika remembered another factor. *Isn't New Way opposed to abortion?* Although Stacey had not said anything about that, Erika thought she remembered reading it when she was researching the agency before interviewing for a placement. *If that's true, then what should I do? Could I get into trouble with New Way for taking a client to have an abortion?*

Erika's confused thoughts were interrupted by Cali, who was again rocking in her chair as she had been in the car. "Gosh," Cali said to no one in particular, "what in the WORLD would I do without Stacey and Lighthouse. I really need to get this abortion . . . If my husband finds out I'm pregnant, he'll kick me outta the house."

Then, looking straight at Erika, Cali said, "I'm so glad you gave me a ride. I don't have anyone else . . . Hey, could you come back with me when the nurse calls me? I'd just feel better if someone else was back there with me, and you seem pretty nice."

Erika felt her stomach twist into knots. "Maybe . . .," she began, feeling that she needed to give Cali some kind of response.

Overlooking Erika' hesitation, Cali turned away and began talking to another patient.

Should I be doing this? Erika wondered. *And what am I supposed to say to her afterwards? How can I help her deal with the abortion if she wants to talk about it? What if she asks me my opinion?*

"When am I going to be seen?" Cali hollered impatiently at the receptionist.

Feeling trapped and embarrassed, Erika thought, *I wish I could just die right here . . . or crawl under the couch.*

A moment later, Cali hollered again, "Can I get some water?"

A fetus is a baby, and abortion is killing. Erika's thoughts raced. *I don't feel comfortable with this. It just doesn't feel right for me. I don't want to support someone who's having an abortion, because I wouldn't do it myself. I had no idea that my own values would end up playing so heavily into this internship, and on only my third day! I mean, is Cali's pregnancy a life or not? When does a fetus become a baby?*

On the other hand, if this is what Cali wants, isn't my job as a social worker to help clients find resources to meet their personal needs and goals? Shouldn't I be fostering Cali's right to self-determination? And what about disappointing Stacey? Plus, Cali already has two children, and it doesn't seem like she's taking care of them. If she does have this baby, it will be addicted to crack because Cali's still using . . . and it probably will be abused all through its childhood. . . . Gosh, what should I do? Cali and Stacey are counting on me . . .

Erika's thoughts were interrupted when the office door opened and a nurse appeared. "Cali Nelson," she called, "you can come on back now."

Cali stood up to go, and then looked at Erika. "C'mon, aren't you coming back with me?"